IDEAS III:

Middle School Physical Activities for a Fit Generation

Editors

Joella Mehrhof
Kathy Ermler

A publication of the National Association for Sport and Physical Education (NASPE)

An association of the American Alliance for Health, Physical Education, Recreation, and Dance (AAHPERD)

1900 Association Drive
Reston, VA   20191-1599
(703) 476-3410
naspe@aahperd.org

ISBN 0-88314-703-3

ABOUT THE EDITORS

JOELLA MEHRHOF is the chairperson of the Division of Health, Physical Education and Recreation at Emporia State University in Emporia, Kansas. She has provided in-service training to numerous school districts in several different states, as well as giving more than 40 presentations at various conferences at the state, regional, national and international level. She is a co-director of the Touch the Future Student Conference; a conference established for the professional development of the top 100 future physical educators in the State of Kansas. Dr. Mehrhof has published eighteen journal articles and three books. She is the co-editor of the Kansas AHPERD Journal.

KATHY ERMLER is an associate professor in the Division of Health, Physical Education and Recreation at Emporia State University in Emporia, Kansas. She is one of the authors and trainers of the Kansas Adolescent Physical Activity and Health Project; a project funded through the Kansas Health Foundation for the improvement and enhancement of secondary physical education and health instruction. Dr. Ermler is one of the founders and directors of the TAKE AIM! Summer Physical Education Conference offered each summer at Emporia State University. She is a well-known presenter and has published numerous professional articles. She is a co-editor of the Kansas AHPERD Journal.

ACKNOWLEDGMENTS

The editors of this publication extend sincere appreciation to all the contributing authors. Without the ideas these authors shared, IDEAS III would not have become a reality. The editors would also like to acknowledge the students at Landon Middle School in Topeka, Kansas who participated in the activities for the photographs in this book.

A special thanks goes to the families and friends of the editors for their support through the long hours of writing and editing.

Joella Mehrhof and Kathy Ermler
Editors

Table of Contents

PREFACE

The middle school physical education program should offer a wide variety of activities that serve as the basis for developing an active and healthy lifestyle. The physical education classroom at the middle school level should provide learning experiences that improve students' fitness levels through games, rhythms, and sports, and help them understand how the body benefits from activity. In addition, it should provide activities and teaching strategies that help students improve self-image and develop decision making skills. *IDEAS III: Middle School Physical Activities for a Fit Generation* is designed to provide activity ideas that can meet these expectations.

The ideas in this book are divided into six major activity categories. They are 1) Fitness Games, 2) Individual Activities, 3) Team Activities, 4) Rhythm and Gymnastics, 5) Initiatives, and 6) Special Events. The activities provided in this book illustrate unique warm-up and conditioning concepts, approaches for the restructuring of traditional games into more successful experiences, and methods for gaining maximum participation.

This book focuses on the teaching and learning process and offers ways to provide a developmentally appropriate curriculum to middle school students. The book suggests that we are "sitting on a gold mine," referring not only to the students as our future, but also to the fact that the physical education profession has tremendous potential for influencing the future.

Joella Mehrhof
Kathy Ermler
Editors

MAXIMIZING PARTICIPATION

The thought of having 30-50 middle school students all active, moving, and using equipment at the same time is enough to make many physical educators check their liability insurance. Maximizing participation is an idea that has long been promoted and accepted in theory. It increases the chance for improvement in both the sport-related skills as well as the health-related components of fitness.

Getting all students active is not a simple process. To translate the theory of maximum participation into practice, teachers may have to change their basic assumptions of class management. Maximizing participation definitely requires more out-of-class preparation and a more creative approach to the use of equipment and facilities. Thus, the following assumptions may need some re-thinking.

Assumption: Use only official boundaries and rules.

Throw out the "official rule book." Students do not need to play on the precise size playing field. The teacher should look at the size of the court or field being used. If it is regulation size, there are probably one or two teams waiting to play. Shorten the boundaries and create more playing areas. Try decreasing the number of students on teams to half the recommended number of the original game.

Assumption: Use only the official equipment of the game.

Students do not need to use the exact piece of equipment to play a game. Due to budgetary constraints, few schools have unlimited numbers of basketballs volleyballs, or rackets. However, by examining the objectives of the lesson, teachers may find that they can achieve the same objective by substituting a different piece of equipment.

Assumption: The type of unit taught or the behavior of the students limits participation.

There may be some classes and some units in which it is dangerous to maximize participation. Some high-risk units like gymnastics, archery, or fencing present specific safety concerns that must be addressed. High-risk units require more structure and supervision than low-risk activities. It may be that the teacher must sacrifice some participation level for a safe and controlled environment. Teachers who have classes that contain students with low levels of maturity and responsibility must exercise more control. In classes that contain students who behave in immature and irresponsible ways, the teacher should attempt to use activities that will improve these qualities, such as group initiatives and team-building activities.

Assumption: Middle school students cannot stay on task unless they are in a very structured environment.

Students need to have experiences in less structured environments. If a tight rein has been kept on the students, the teacher will be doomed to failure, when, all of a sudden, the students are expected to function with less structure and control. Teachers should assess their current class structure. If the students are always in line with only minimal use of equipment, it will be difficult to give every student a ball and expect on-task behavior. The students do not know how to behave or what is expected of them in this type of structure.

It may be necessary to wean students from a highly structured environment to one with less structure. If limited amounts of equipment have been used, begin to increase the amount. Eventually work the class into activity groups of two or three students. It is important during this process to state or post the expectations of the students. Another method off easing into a less structured environment is the use of circuits. With circuits, several stations may be used. A small number of students are place d in each group in order that every student has use of a ball, jump rope, racket, etc.

Maximizing participation does not have to result in a chaotic environment. The more opportunities students have to be active, the more likely they are to increase their fitness levels and improve their skill. In addition, students may begin to take more responsibility for their own learning and may become more self-directed. If teachers are willing to change their basic assumptions about class management, they may find that this change can contribute significantly to the growth of their students.

Fun Facts About Exercise and the Body

Smaller than a bread box - The heart is a hollow muscular organ that is roughly the size of a man's fist, averaging approximately five inches in length. It weighs about 10.5 ounces in males and 8.75 ounces in females.

Lite stuff - Your lungs are light enough to float on water.

Buddy, can you spare a part? Although you can't just go to a human spare parts store to buy a new replacements for a body organ, organ transplants take place every day. The cost of a transplant to replace either your heart or lung is about $100,000.

The breath of life - The average human inhales approximately 3,500 gallons of air daily.

Six quarts low - If you run a 100-yard dash, you'll need about seven quarts of oxygen. Since you only have about one quart available in your blood, you'll have to supply the rest by rapid breathing.

On and on and on - Placed end to end, the blood vessels in your body would stretch almost three times around the equator.

Thinner than thin - The tiniest blood vessels in your body, known as capillaries, are 50 times thinner than the finest human hair.

The sound of silence - A heartbeat can't be heard. When you listen to someone's heart, the sound you hear is the closing of the heart's valves. A heartbeat itself is a silent contraction of the muscles.

When push comes to shove - Your blood rushes through your arteries with enough pressure to lift a column of blood five feet into the air.

No, thank you, I'm full - If you are 25 pounds overweight, you have nearly 5,000 extra miles of blood vessels through which your heart must pump blood.

Keep your left up - A knockout in boxing occurs when a boxer is hit by a forceful blow that causes a chain reaction in the circulatory system. This reaction ultimately causes the supply of blood in the heart, lungs, and brain to pool in the boxer's abdomen, and to decrease the circulation in the brain, resulting in a loss of consciousness.

Almost as fast as a speeding bullet - It only takes about 23 seconds for blood to circulate through your entire body.

Taking a break - Your heart rests between beats. If the length of time of these rests over your lifetime were added up, you would find that your heart stands still for about 20 years.

True blue - Inside your body, your blood is blue. Blood turns red only when it mixes with oxygen, which is what occurs when you cut yourself and bleed.

Keep them coming - Every second, your body manufactures 2.5 million new red blood cells. During the period of a month, all your red blood cells are replaced with new ones.

Avoid a false reading - The best spot for taking your pulse following heavy exercise is your wrist. Pressure on your carotid artery (at the neck) can slow your heart rate, thereby giving you a false reading on the intensity level of your workout.

A systematic slow down - Your resting heart rate decreases approximately one beat per minute every one to two weeks of aerobic conditioning for the first 10 to 20 weeks of training.

Lung power lapse - Your breathing capacity decreases as you age (i.e., the total volume of oxygen inhaled with each breath declines). For example, the oxygen intake of an individual over the age of 80 is only half that of someone under 30.

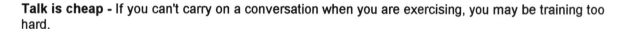

Lung power - Aerobic training improves the condition and efficiency of your breathing muscles so that your body can utilize more lung capacity during exercise.

When less is more - An aerobically fit (trained) individual uses fewer breaths to move the same amount of air.

Talk is cheap - If you can't carry on a conversation when you are exercising, you may be training too hard.

More than a few - The human body has more than 650 muscles.

A miniature Charles Atlas - Muscles are comprised of muscle fibers. Each fiber is thinner than human hair and can support up to 1,000 times its own weight.

Recipe for success - The American College of Sports Medicine recommends a strength-training program that includes a minimum of one set (eight to 12 repetitions) of eight to IO exercises that condition the major muscles groups, performed at least two days per week.

Where did the strength go? By the age of 65, individuals who haven't engaged in exercise on a regular basis may incur a decrease in their muscular strength level by as much as 80 percent.

It's all or nothing - When an individual muscle fiber is stimulated, it contracts to its fullest extent.

Beyond your control - How much an individual can lift is influenced by at least seven factors: strength-training program intensity, predominant muscle fiber type, hormonal levels, body proportions, tendon insertion points, muscle-tendon ratios, and neurological efficiency.

How much is more - All other factors being equal, an individual who moves 200 pounds a distance of two feet has done more than a person who lifts 300 pounds one foot.

Yes, she can - Women can and should get strong. Since the admission of women to West Point in 1976, for example, that institution has had several women graduates who could perform more than 100 straight-back push-ups in two minutes, including one woman in 1990 who did 132 pushups in two minutes.

Training for a purpose - The basic strength training methods are generally grouped into five classifications: isometric (you contract your muscle, but the involved joints don't move); isotonic (the amount of external resistance does not vary while you are exercising); eccentric-only (exercise involving muscular contractions in which the muscle only lengthens); isokinetic (exercise which involves a constant rate of speed of movement); and variable resistance (exercise in which the resistance accommodates to the strength curve of the muscle being stressed).

Gone, but not forgotten - By the age of 80, sedentary individuals will lose about half of their muscle mass.

Unique in its own way - No two muscles in your body have exactly the same function. When any one muscle is paralyzed, either stability of the body part is impaired or some specific movement is lost.

The recipe for making skeletal muscles - Approximately 75 percent of skeletal muscle is water, 20 percent is protein, and the remaining 5 percent is made up of inorganic salts and other substances.

The "meat" of the matter - Extra protein will not enhance your efforts to build larger muscles. Your body is unable to store protein. If you consume protein in excess of your caloric and protein needs, any extra protein will either be excreted or converted and stored as fat.

The time of your life - Maximum strength of men and women is generally achieved between the ages of 20 and 30.

A breath of common sense - Breathing properly is a basic safety consideration while strength training. A fundamental precept to which you should always adhere is to never hold your breath while strength training. Holding your breath results in a potentially dangerous build-up of intrathoracic pressure. This pressure (inside your rib cage) compresses the right side of your heart, which in turn, restricts the flow of blood and oxygen to your entire body.

Balancing act - Your strength-training program should emphasize muscle balance. In your body, you have muscles that oppose each other (e.g., your quadriceps muscles are opposed by your hamstring muscles). These muscles have a proportional strength relationship between them. If one is much stronger than the other, you run the risk of injuring the weaker muscle.

Source - Peterson, J., Bryant, C., and Hagen, R. - **Internet**

IDEAS III:

Section One

Fitness Games

ATHLETIC AEROBIC CIRCUIT

By Linda Wilkins
FiTrain
Acworth, GA

National Standards

✐ Exhibits a physically active lifestyle.
✐ Achieves and maintains a health-enhancing level of physical fitness.
✐ Understands that physical activity provides the opportunity for enjoyment, challenge, self-expression, and social interaction.

Introduction

The athletic aerobic circuit is a great way to incorporate a variety of skills into an activity in which everyone in the class can participate successfully. The self-paced nature of this circuit permits each student to work at his/her appropriate skill and fitness level. Students, regardless of skill level, can have fun and develop a sense of teamwork and camaraderie.

Aerobic Stations

Divide the class into four groups. Each group will be at each station for a total of eight minutes. During these eight minutes the students will perform an aerobic activity for three minutes, an interval activity for one minute, another aerobic activity for three more minutes, and a muscular strength activity for one minute. Remind students they should work at a moderate pace during the aerobic portions of each station and then give 100% during the one-minute interval training. The teacher should travel among the stations to provide verbal incentives and hands-on skill teaching.

Stations may vary depending on equipment availability, number of students, and location the of activity. A four station example follows:

	Aerobic (3 minutes)	Interval (1 minute)	Aerobic (3 minutes)	Strength (1 minute)
Station I	Basic bench step (Step up, up, down, down)	Jump rope	Knee lift step (Step up, knee up, step down, down)	Triceps dips

(Equipment: step benches, jump ropes)

Station II	Basic slide	Speed skate	Slide squat	Push-ups

(Equipment: aerobic slides [or paper plates on floor)

Station III	Ball dribbling between cones	Sprints	Partner ball passing	Squats

Equipment: balls, cones)

Station IV	Straddle down (Start on top of bench, step down, down on opposite side of bench - step up, up)	Quick footwork drills	Lunges from the top of step with weights (Use both legs)	Biceps curls with weights

(Equipment: steps, weights)

At the end of the eighth minute and the conclusion of the first station, each group moves to the next station. After the students have rotated through all four stations, the class may conclude with all students jogging for three minutes. Follow the jogging with some abdominal work and a flexibility cool-down.

One key to keeping everyone on task is the music. It is helpful to format a cassette tape for the workout time. The method of formatting a cassette tape for the circuit follows:

Activity	Time	Beats per Minute
Warm Up	5-8 minutes	130-140
Break to Stations	*20 seconds*	
Aerobic	3 minutes	120-130
Break	*4-10 seconds*	
Interval	1 minute	145-160
Break	*4-10 seconds*	
Aerobic	3 minutes	120-130
Break	*4- 1 0 seconds*	
Strength	1 minute	110-130
Break	*20 seconds*	

(Repeat the Aerobic, Interval, Aerobic, Strength with the breaks for three additional times with different music but the same tempos)

Jogging	3 minutes	145-160
Abdominal	3-5 minutes	110-130
Flexibility	3-5 minutes	<110

The short musical cuts on the compact disc, _Jock Rock_, are perfect as cues to let your students know that it's time to change activity or station. Use the shorter cuts to change activity within a station and the longer cuts to change stations.

Conclusion

Variations of these stations can be used with individuals or groups as necessary. For example, if the group at Station I is getting bored with doing a basic step, change the move to a turn step or running step. Activities at the stations are limited only by the imagination! Movements during the three-minute aerobic segments can be changed as often as needed. For example, at Station 1, the students might do a basic step for one minute, followed by a turn step for one minute, followed by over the top step for one minute. If the students are well versed in appropriate moves, allow them to take turns choosing the aerobic movement. If training an athletic team, stations can be more sports-specific than the general circuit illustrated.

FITNESS FUN ON THE RUN

By Mark Stanbrough
Emporia State University
Emporia, KS

National Standards

🖉 Exhibits a physically active lifestyle.
🖉 Achieves and maintains a health-enhancing level of physical fitness
🖉 Understands that physical activity provides the opportunity for enjoyment, challenge, self-expression and social interaction

Introduction

One of the most important components of physical fitness is cardiovascular endurance. One activity that can develop cardiovascular endurance is running. However, many students, neither enjoy nor are motivated by running. Fitness Fun on the Run activities are attractive alternatives to the traditional method of running laps.

Before participating in any of these activities, the students should be sufficiently warmed-up to prepare the body for the activity. For example, students could jog to a station, perform a required task, and jog back to the starting area. After the general body warm-up the students should stretch. During the latter part of stretching, the teacher could give instructions and pass out any materials needed for the activities.

General Guidelines for All Activities

1. Students may participate as individuals, with a partner, or as a member of a team. If the partner option is chosen, the partners could run together the entire way or have the partners divide the stations any way they choose. This allows the students to plan what stations they will perform. Often, the faster runners will select the stations that are further away and require more running. Teams can be required to run together or they can divide the tasks.

2. These activities can be done for time, used as a race, a predictive event, or simply as a participation activity.

3. Set a time limit on all activities. If someone has not accomplished the task by the end of the time period he/she, should report back to the teacher.

4. It takes some planning to determine the direction of the running in many of these activities. In some activities, there is no prescribed course or sequencing of stations, so the students have to plan how they can accomplish the task in the most efficient manner. Emphasize to the students that if they plan their course before the run, they will benefit from this planning in the long run.

5. Safety should be stressed at all times. If the course has any dangerous obstacles, these should be addressed before the students begin the activity. Remember to emphasize the boundaries of the course.

Stump Jumpers Run

Students receive a map of the area that contains approximately 10 stations marked with an X. Students run to an area marked with an X on the map. At each station there is a color coded marking pen. Students mark over the X with the colored marking pen. When the students have run to all 10 different stations on their map, they return to the starting line.

There is no prescribed course or order of stations. Students are instructed to run to each station in the most efficient manner. The teacher notes the finish time and then checks the map for the 10 different colored marks. If the students do not have all 10 marks and the time limit has not expired, they are sent back on the course to find the missing stations.

Explorer Run

Before class, the teacher should develop a series of questions about the buildings and landmarks on the school grounds. Students must run to the various landmarks and then answer the questions about each landmark. They do not have to visit the landmarks in any particular order. After they have visited all landmarks, the students should return to the starting point and have the teacher check their answers. If they are not correct and time has not expired, they return for more information. Examples of clues that can be developed about the landmarks on school grounds include:

- How many flagpoles are there on the school grounds? How many doors are on the west side of the school?
- How many windows are on the outside of the school?
- How many swings are on the playground?
- What is written on the front of the main school building?
- How many fence posts are there on the school grounds?

Clue Run

This is an excellent activity to do in groups of two or three. The objective of the clue run is to have the students figure out the location the clue is describing. They run to that location and find a box containing a new clue. The students go from clue to clue until they arrive at the grand or final location. The teacher should collect the clue slips in order to verify that the students have been to all the clues. Some examples of locations on your school grounds and clues that can be used for these locations include:

Swings:

Going high, going low,
Hanging still when no one's there,
Go with the flow,
Back and forth as the wind blows your hair.

Head of nature trail:

Back to nature where the weeds are high,
At the head, look down, not toward the sky.

Basketball goal

Shoot for the sky, but not too high
10 feet tall, ball and all.

Softball field:

Hit a double, don't have to slide,
On the ground, you'd tear your hide.

Trivia Run

Set up a 10 station running course on the school grounds. The students must jog to each station on the course. At each station the students stop and attempt to answer a trivia question. In addition, they need to complete the exercise at the station. For example, the exercise at station 1 may be push-ups, at station 2 it might be sit-ups. Students write the answer to the trivia question down on a card that they carry with them. When all teams have finished the course, the teacher provides them with the correct answer to each trivia question. The trivia questions could focus on topics students are studying in physical education or other academic areas. The questions might also be centered on a common theme being studied by the entire school (e.g., The Olympic Games). The following questions are examples of trivia questions and stations that could be used. Notice that all the answers to the trivia questions are numbers. If a student's answer to the first question was 1960, and since he was not correct, he would do 8 additional push-ups (1968 - 1960 = 8). If a student's answer to question five was 2 gold medals, then he/she would do 5 additional 30 yard sprints (7 - 2 = 5).

Trivia Olympics

Exercise	Trivia Question	Answer
#1-Push-ups (10x)	What year were the Mexico City Olympics held?	1968
#2-Sit-ups (15x)	What year were the Winter Olympics last held in Lake Placid, NY?	1980
#3-Flex & jump (10x)	What year were the Olympics held in Melbourne, Australia?	1956
#4-Squat thrusts (10x)	Jesse Owens won how many Olympic Medals in 1936?	4
#5-30 yd. Sprints (2x)	How many gold medals did Mark Spitz win in 1972?	7
#6-Jump rope (50x)	In what year did the first modern day Olympics take place?	1896
#7-Jumping jacks (25x)	Age at which Nadia Commanci won gold?	14
#8-Tuck jumps (5x)	First year U.S. men's basketball team lost gold?	1972

Conclusion

Cardiovascular endurance is an important component of fitness. While running might be an excellent way of developing this component, many students find it painful and boring. The Fitness Fun on the Run activities are ways to distract students and provide challenges to motivate them.

**Health-Related
Fitness Testing**

Health-Related Fitness Testing Stations

**By Pug Parris
Abilene University
Abilene, TX**

National Standards

- Applies movement concepts and principles to the learning and development of motor skills.
- Exhibits a physically active lifestyle.
- Achieves and maintains a health-enhancing level of physical fitness.

Introduction

Physical fitness evaluation produces some management problems for the physical educator. Testing creates a long line of students who are waiting to get tested due to lack of testing personnel or testing equipment. This waiting diminishes maximum participation and causes the students who are waiting to decrease body core temperature. This decrease in temperature will lead to a reduced performance on the health-related component being tested.

By converting the testing protocol into a station activity, the middle school physical educator will lessen management problems, improve student performance, and provide students with fitness workout. The following class organization plan demonstrates how the sit-and-reach flexibility test can be incorporated into station activity.

Class Management Suggestions

After a brief class warm-up, students are assigned a starting place in the circuit (somewhere between station 1-22). The students are at each station for one minute before moving to the next station. This allows a student at least three minutes of warm-up before engaging in stretching. This starting point is where students who did not have a starting point station enter the rotation.

The success of station activity depends on preparing the gym ahead of time with sequential signs that describe the nature of the activity for that given station. Pictures, photocopies from textbook, or simple sketches enhance understanding and remind the student of the exact nature of the activity.

Prior to class, the teacher should prepare a tape with appropriate music that ranges between 128-140 beats per minute. A tape should be developed with a minimum of 46 one-minute segments. Experience with middle school students indicates that using different songs for each segment generates student enthusiasm. This tape will guide the rotation system for the station activity.

Strength Stations

Successful strength training progression includes five stations:

1. Seated biceps curls.
2. Curl-ups or crunches.
3. Upright rows with hand weights or resistance tubing.
4. Overhead presses with weights or tubing.
5. Hula hooping.

The latter is not so much to serve as a strength training activity but to get students physically prepared to enter the next 20 aerobic stations.

Aerobic Stations

The next 20 stations are aerobic in nature. Sample activities for these aerobic stations include:

- Jogging (in place or in a small designated area)
- Jumping rope (with all the many variations)
- Bench stepping (lead with right leg at one station and left at another)
- Stair climbing on bleachers
- Stationary bike riding (if equipment is available)
- Board sliding (if equipment is available)

The last aerobic station (station #25) should be a monitoring point with a towel (to wipe off sweat), a pulse measurement device (such as hand-held monitors), and a clipboard (with a sign-in sheet) for recording beats-per-minute. Students should record their working heart rate and continue to walk around and read the monitor. In the absence of a measurement device, the students could figure beats-per-minute with a watch.

Stretching Stations

After this final aerobic station, the students move into five minutes of stretching (stations 26-30). A recommended progression is:

Stretching Station 1: Standing. Achilles tendon and calf stretches against wall.

Stretching Station 2: Tailor sitting with one leg then the other in front.

Stretching Station 3: Hamstring stretches with both legs while lying on the back.

Stretching Station 4: Modified hurdler's stretches with both legs while seated and finally, approximating the sit-and-reach.

Stretching Station 5: Observation. Each student should watch the person before him/her doing the sit-and-reach in order to understand the procedures.

Stretching Station 6: Sit-and-Reach. With the teacher administering the test, the student does his/her attempts efficiently and with proper form. The teacher or a student assistant records the data. This station should be positioned so that the teacher has a full view of all the class activity and can monitor on-task and off-task behaviors. Students should remove shoes before performing the sit-and-reach.

Stretching Station 7: Put shoes back on. After this station, the student re-enters the cycle at the strength development portion with seated biceps curl and continues around until the teacher has finished rotations for the entire group.

Conclusion

Although the sit-and-reach test was illustrated in this article, this type of testing protocol can be used with any of the health-related fitness components. Three main principles apply to using a station activity format for the testing:

❶ Students are not waiting for a chance to perform the test, since only one student enters the testing station at a time.

❷ Five minutes of strength development and five minutes of stretching compliment the 20 minute cardiovascular activity session.

❸ The body's core temperature has risen prior to testing. This station plan requires the students to complete anywhere from 3 to 20 one-minute aerobic stations prior to the test.

This plan should not be an impromptu lesson. The prudent educator would work up to any station activity where individual pacing is important by first spending several days working the activities into the performance repertoire of the students.

LEARNING INTENSITY LEVEL OF AEROBIC EXERCISE

By Mark Stanbrough
Emporia State University
Emporia, KS

National Standards

✐ Applies movement concepts and principles to the learning and development of motor skills.
✐ Exhibits a physically active lifestyle.
✐ Achieves and maintains a health-enhancing level of physical fitness

Introduction

On your mark, get set, go! You have just sent your students off for a run. Most students feel great for the first several yards. After a matter of seconds, the big bear associated with anaerobic work attacks and the students begin to feel fatigued. Students need to learn to pace themselves to receive the optimal benefits of aerobic workouts and decrease the negative effects associated with this type of exercise. Teachers can use aerobic target zone and the activities listed under ratings of perceived exertion exercises to help students pace themselves and improve cardiovascular fitness.

Aerobic target zone is the moderate exercise level at which students are able to continue exercising for an extended period of time. Students should understand that if they exercise at this intensity level, they will develop stronger and healthier hearts. Exercise above the target zone is anaerobic and can not be continued for long periods of time. Exercise below the target zone is better than no exercise, but it does not build optimal levels of fitness.

Determining the Aerobic Target Zone

To determine the aerobic target zone, the student must determine the maximal heart rate (MHR) by using the simple formula of 220 -12 (age) to get an estimate of the maximal heart rate. In addition, the student should determine the lower and upper limits of the aerobic target zone. The lower limit is calculated at 60% of the maximal heart rate (.6 x MHR) and the upper limit is calculated at 85% of the maximal heart rate (.85 x MHR). For middle school students the aerobic target zone ranges from 124 to 175 beats per minute.

Once the students know their target zone, they must learn to take their heart rate during exercise. Heart rate monitors can be used to take the pulse rates. However, if these monitors are not available, students may use the manual method of determining heart rate. To find the heart rate manually, have the students place the fingertips of the index and middle fingers over the carotid or radial artery. They should move their fingers around this area until they feel a strong pulse. They should take their pulse immediately after they exercise. Tell them to press gently because pressing too hard on the carotid artery could cause-a reflex action that will slow the heart rate. They should learn to locate the pulse quickly and count for six seconds. Take that number and add a zero to the end of it (e.g., 15 beats in 6 seconds + 0 = 150 beats per minute). This will give the student the estimated heart rate for one minute.

Rating of Perceived Exertion

When beginning a program, it is very important to monitor heart rate to determine intensity level. Once students become experienced with aerobic target zone efforts, they can begin to gauge their intensity level based on perceived exertion. Ratings of perceived exertion are listed in chart.

Rating of Perceived Exertion	
1	very, very light
2	very light
3	fairly light
4	slightly moderate
5	moderate
6	above moderate
7	hard
8	very hard
9	very, very hard
10	extremely hard

Exercise 7

a. Jump rope at a slow pace for 30 seconds.
b. Count your heart rate for 6 seconds, add 0, and record it. _____
c. Rate the intensity of the exercise by using the perceived exertion scale. _____

Exercise 8

a. Jump rope at a medium pace for 30 seconds.
b. Count your heart rate for 6 seconds, add 0, and record it. _____
c. Rate the intensity of the exercise by using the perceived exertion scale. _____

Exercise 9

a. Jump rope at a pace that will put you in your target zone.
b. Count your heart rate for 6 seconds, add 0, and record it. _____
c. Rate the intensity of the exercise by using the perceived exertion scale. _____

**If you were above your target zone, slow down on the next exercise.
If you were below your target zone, speed up and if you are in your
target zone, keep the pace.**

Conclusion

These activities will help your students become aware of the pace at which they need to exercise to be in their aerobic target zone. When students are working in their target zone, students should rate their perceived exertion from 4 to 7. By learning the effort needed to exercise in the aerobic target zone, students become more knowledgeable about how to exercise. This knowledge can extend through a lifetime, as students realize that exercise is enjoyable and not painful.

References

Borg, G. (1982). Psychophysical Bases of Perceived Exertion. *Medicine and Science in Sports and Science.*
Stanbrough, M.E. (1994). *Lifetime Fitness.* Dubuque, IA: Kendall-Hunt Publishing Co.

Exercise 7

a. Jump rope at a slow pace for 30 seconds.
b. Count your heart rate for 6 seconds, add 0, and record it. _____
c. Rate the intensity of the exercise by using the perceived exertion scale. _____

Exercise 8

a. Jump rope at a medium pace for 30 seconds.
b. Count your heart rate for 6 seconds, add 0, and record it. _____
c. Rate the intensity of the exercise by using the perceived exertion scale. _____

Exercise 9

a. Jump rope at a pace that will put you in your target zone.
b. Count your heart rate for 6 seconds, add 0, and record it. _____
c. Rate the intensity of the exercise by using the perceived exertion scale. _____

If you were above your target zone, slow down on the next exercise. If you were below your target zone, speed up and if you are in your target zone, keep the pace.

Conclusion

These activities will help your students become aware of the pace at which they need to exercise to be in their aerobic target zone. When students are working in their target zone, students should rate their perceived exertion from 4 to 7. By learning the effort needed to exercise in the aerobic target zone, students become more knowledgeable about how to exercise. This knowledge can extend through a lifetime, as students realize that exercise is enjoyable and not painful.

References

Borg, G. (1982). Psychophysical Bases of Perceived Exertion. *Medicine and Science in Sports and Science.*

Stanbrough, M.E. (1994). *Lifetime Fitness.* Dubuque, IA: Kendall-Hunt Publishing Co.

Physical Fitness Routines for Middle School Students

By Paul W. Darst, Robert Pangrazi,
and Belinda Stillwell
Arizona State University
Tempe, AZ

National Standards

- Exhibits a physically active lifestyle.
- Achieves and maintains a health-enhancing level of physical fitness.
- Understands that physical activity provides the opportunity for enjoyment, challenge, self-expression, and social interaction.

Introduction

Middle school can be a difficult time for many students because of the tremendous changes taking place in their lives. Students move through changes in their physical, social, emotional, and intellectual characteristics. There often is a rapid and uneven growth spurt during this time. Social and emotional challenges with peers and authority figures place high demands on their capabilities. New and difficult academic and intellectual situations occur regularly.

With this in mind, it is important that middle school physical educators consider the unique characteristics, abilities, interests, and developmental levels of these students. The middle school experience can be one of the most important links in the total school curriculum because students make personal decisions about what they like and dislike. The decisions the students make often are irreversible and last a lifetime. For this reason, everything possible should be done to keep students excited about and interested in physical activity.

Novel physical fitness activities and a variety of teaching strategies can be set up in an enjoyable and challenging manner. Music can be added in a number of positive ways that students will enjoy. There should be a strong focus on lifetime activities and the health-related components of physical fitness.

Circuit Training Activities with Jogging

A fitness circuit is set up using laminated cards with a paper loop stapled on the back of the card. Each card is placed on a boundary cone at each station. The stations should include a variety of muscle groups and components of physical fitness. The stations should include exercise equipment and activities such as dyna-bands, jump rope activities, and partner-resistance activities.

Music tapes should be prepared with 30 seconds of music and 20 seconds of silence. The music cues the students to begin exercising at the station activities. When the music stops, the students take a jog all the way around the cones and then move up one station.

Cooperative Exercise Hunts

Students work together in teams. The teams stay together and "hunt" for the exercise area of the gym or field space. The teams are given a laminated card that lists the areas to find and the activities to perform at the designated areas. The sheets could have 6-10 activities depending on the length of the fitness segment. Each group is assigned a different starting point to ensure students are spread across all areas and that a back-up does not occur at one of the fitness areas. Examples of entries on the exercise card include:

1. Leap frog to each corner of the gym and perform curl-ups for 30 seconds. All team members should work together.
2. Run to the open set of bleachers and perform step-ups on the first row for 30 seconds.

3. Perform at least five triceps push-ups together as a group.
4. Carioca step to each of the other groups and tell them that they are doing a good job.
5. Jog as a group to six people wearing something red.
6. Run and find the short jump ropes. Complete as many jumps as you can in 20 seconds.
7. Slide and touch six walls, two different red lines, and three different black lines. Stay together with your group.
8. Jog to the "jumping jacks" sign and perform jumping jacks for 30 seconds using at least four different variations in arm or foot patterns.
9. Crab walk the width of the gym with your group.

Fitness Cookie Jar Exchange

A variety of fitness activities are written on different index cards and then placed in a "cookie jar" (shoe box). The shoe box is placed at a convenient place for students to pick up and return the cards. Students work with a partner. The activities include primarily fitness activities, but could include ball handling skills or other manipulative skills in a specific area. Examples include the following:

1 Play catch with a frisbee using at least two different types of throws and catches.
2. Bear crawl the width of the gym.
3. Jog and shake hands with 10 different people. Tell them to have a good day.
4. Perform two free throw shots at two different baskets.
5. Defensive slide to four students wearing blue.
6. Carioca step around the basketball court.
7. Skip backward with your partner and touch three walls.
8. Perform three partner resistance exercises

Music can be programmed on a tape for 30 second intervals to structure the transitions for students. A 10 second interval without music could be used for getting a new card. Students perform as many repetitions as possible while the music is playing. This allows more individualization for students with varying fitness and skill abilities. Students should be encouraged to do as many stations as possible.

Partner Racetrack Fitness

Students work with a partner at one of the established stations. The stations are arranged in a circle or rectangle around the area. Each station has a sign with five or six exercises. On the start signal, one partner begins the first exercise on the card while the other partner jogs around the perimeter of the stations. Upon returning, the partners switch roles and the former jogger does the next task listed on the card. The teacher can also change the locomotor movement for the students going around the cones. Continuous music can be used to motivate the students.

Long Jump Rope Fitness Routine

Students are in groups of three with a long jump rope. Two students are turning the rope and the third student is the jumper. When the music starts, the jumper makes three jumps and begins running a figure eight around the turners. The jumper makes three jumps each time that he/she enters the center of the figure eight. The focus is on entering the turning rope and making the three jumps and then continuing on to the figure eight. When the music stops, a new jumper starts and the old jumper becomes a turner. The music should be programmed for 45 seconds of music and 15 seconds of silence for change time.

Conclusion

Middle school students can be challenged to improve their fitness levels through various physical activities. Working with partners or in small groups at this level is recommended. The use of music can also provide motivation.

PFT - Personal Fitness Time: Creating a Fitness Foundation for the Future

By Wendall J. Brown
Brownfield High School
Brownfield, TX

National Standards

🖎 Exhibits a physically active lifestyle.
🖎 Achieves and maintains a health-enhancing level of physical fitness.
🖎 Demonstrates responsible personal and social behavior in physical activity settings.

Introduction

Personal fitness is an important outcome of any physical education program. Fitness should be emphasized throughout the curriculum, regardless of the unit or activity being covered. Students cannot participate or develop basic skills in any activity if they do not have sufficient muscular strength, muscular endurance, or cardiovascular endurance.

In most physical education classes, students have a wide variety of fitness levels. To accommodate these various levels, an effort should be made to create an environment that meets the individual fitness needs of all the students. One way these needs can be met within a structured physical education class is by instituting a personal fitness time (PFT) program.

PFT Program

Prior to the initiation of the PFT program, students are tested and measured on various physiological and fitness parameters. Height, weight, and blood pressure readings are taken and recorded on a chart. This information is then placed in each student's folder. In addition, students measure their

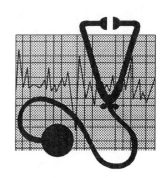

chest, calves, biceps, thighs, waist, and hips. Body composition is assessed through the use of skin fold calipers. This data becomes the basis for students to establish and develop their own personal fitness goals.

Every student participates in the PFT program for the first 30 minutes of every class period. (This time can be adjusted up or down depending upon your class time.) Based on the results of the fitness testing, the students establish fitness goals and then select one of several activity options. While a totally individualized physical education program is not possible, students may select from several structured choices.

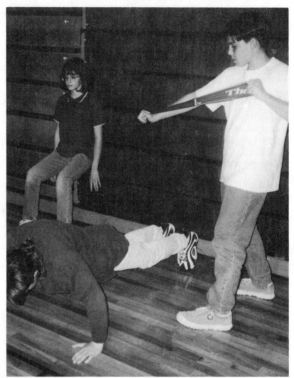

The activity selections are designed in packages that ensure that, no matter what package is selected, all students will receive a total body workout. Packages are established for low, moderate, and high fitness levels. Each of the structured packages includes activities that will develop cardiovascular endurance, muscular strength/endurance, and flexibility. The activities include: running, fitness walking, agility movements, jump roping, step aerobics, push-ups, sit-ups, sprinting, and muscular strength activities.

Each student is taught the proper technique for all the activities in each package before implementing the individual assessment program. Students are required to keep a notebook for their log sheets, handouts, and tests. The notebooks are kept in the gym and are accessible to the students during class time. The log sheets also have areas for recording times and/or levels of achievement for each activity. The students are reminded regularly to compare their efforts to those of previous attempts.

It is hoped this comparison will enhance intrinsic motivation. The log sheets are checked periodically to assure that students are tracking their progress properly. There is no advantage in recording inaccurate scores because no student-to-student comparisons are made. Students retake physical tests and measurements to establish new personal bests every nine weeks. Students are asked to evaluate their fitness goals and to offer written explanations or why the goals were achieved or not achieved. New goals are then set and a new training period is started.

Monitoring Student Progress

Implementing a program similar to this one takes a little time to organize, but the benefits of this plan are tremendous. Monitoring the students during clasp requires the instructor to continually move throughout the workout area. Students must understand that PFT is a privilege that provides them with an opportunity to be responsible and mature. It is not necessary, however, to assume a dictatorial attitude toward the students. The program needs to be implemented slowly; use one area at a time until the students understand what is expected of them.

Conclusion

Students appreciate the responsibility given to them and respond positively. Students' attitudes are much better about fitness activities since they enjoy the control this program gives them. The students also enjoy not having to compete with everyone else in the class. Self-esteem is increased because the rewards are mostly intrinsic.

Level 1: Low-Level Fitness Program

(Choose 1 option)

Power walking a one-mile outside course
- Upon completion of the walk, students take and record their pulse.
- Students complete a 30-second sit-up and push-up test and record the results.
- The exercise sheet is signed by their partner.
- Students must then do 3 sets of 10 biceps curls, and 2 sets of 20-second wall sits.

Circuit
- Walk 5 laps around the walking track (approximately ½ mile).
- 30 steps each leg on 12" step test bench (check pulse and record on sheet).
- 2 sets of 10 curl-ups.
- 4 shuffles down long side of gym floor, right leg leading.
- 4 shuffles down long side of gym floor, left leg leading.
- 2 sets of 8 push-ups.
- 30 jump ropes.
- 3 sets of 10 biceps curls with resistive bands or hand weights.
- 2 sets of 20-second wall sits.

3 minutes of cool down stretch

Level 2: Moderate-Level Fitness Program

(Choose 1 option)

Jog a one-mile outside course
- Upon completion of the run, students take and record their pulse.
- Students complete a 20-second sit-up and push-up test and record results.
- The exercise sheet is signed by their partner.
- Students must then do 40 jump ropes, 3 sets of 10 biceps curls, and 2 sets of 20-second wall sits.

Circuit
- Jog 10 laps in the gym.
- Sprint 6 lengths of the gym floor.
- 40 jump ropes.
- Check pulse and record.
- 2 sets of 12 curl-ups.
- 4 shuffles down long side of gym floor, right leg leading.
- 4 shuffles down long side of gym floor, left leg leading.
- 2 sets of 10 push-ups.
- 3 sets of 10 biceps curls.
- 3 sets of 20-second wall sits.
- 30 steps each leg on 12" step test bench.

Step video aerobics
- The step video is done for 20 minutes.
- Pulse rates are taken and recorded.
- Students complete a 30-second sit-up and push-up test and record the results.
- The exercise sheet is signed by their partner.
- Students do 40 jump ropes, 3 sets of 10 biceps curls, and 2 sets of 20-second wall sits.

3 minutes of cool down stretch

Level 3: High-Level Fitness Program

(Choose 1 option)

Jog a one-mile outside course
➡ These students all have personal mile bests of less than 8 minutes for the men and 9 minutes for the women.
➡ Upon completion of the jog students take and record their pulse.
➡ Students complete a 30-second sit-up and push-up test and record the results.
➡ The exercise sheet is signed by partner.
➡ Students must then do 4 sprints the length of the gym floor, 4 lateral shuffles the length of the gym floor, 3 sets of 10 biceps curls, and 2 sets of 20-second wall sits.

Circuit
➡ 6 shuffles down long side of gym floor, right leg leading.
➡ 6 shuffles down long side of gym floor, left leg leading.
➡ Jog 15 laps in the gym.
➡ Sprint 6 lengths of the gym.
➡ Check pulse and record.
➡ 2 sets of 15 push-ups.
➡ 3 sets of 10 biceps curls.
➡ 3 sets of 12 curl-ups.
➡ 3 sets of 20-second wall sits.
➡ 30 steps each leg on a 12" step test bench.
➡ 30 jump ropes.

3 minutes of cool down stretch

INCORPORATING TECHNOLOGY INTO YOUR MIDDLE SCHOOL PHYSICAL EDUCATION PROGRAM

By Mark Stanbrough
Emporia State University
Emporia, KS

National Standards

✎ Applies movement concepts and principles to the learning and development of motor skills.

Introduction

Technology-assisted instruction involves instruction with the computer or some other type of technology in order to enhance the learning process. Technology is not a passing fad, but will continue to influence education in the future.

Many physical educators are uncertain as to the way in which technology can be utilized in the physical education environment. In order to successfully integrate technology into the physical education class, a teacher must begin by identifying the instructional objective for the class. Once the objective is established, the teacher should select appropriate hardware and software will facilitate this objective. The purpose of this article is to present several ideas that may assist the physical educator in introducing technology into a physical activity setting.

Technology Stations

Technology can be easily worked into a physical education class by setting up technology stations. These stations can incorporate other skill or fitness stations used during the lesson. Examples of possible stations include:

🖨 Videotape station that has a short (1 minute) skill lesson (e.g., golf swing, tennis serve, lifting technique).

📟 Videotape camera - students perform a skill and are videotaped performing the skill (at different time, the students can view and evaluate their performance).

📟 Muscle station - computer program is set up to introduce or review muscles being used during activity.

Activity and Food Analysis

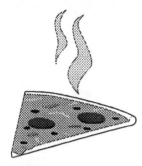

Using a computer software program, students may calculate caloric expenditure or analyze their nutritional levels. Examples of activity and food analysis programs include *Dine Healthy*, *Nutritionist*, and *EHSA Research Food Processor*. Sample activity and food analysis questions are listed in Table 1.

Table I
Activity and Nutritional Questions

Activity Questions

Determine the number of calories you expended in your physical education class. Include your warm-up, workout, and cool-down. _____

How many calories would you use if you:

Ran a mile in 7 minutes	_____
Walked a mile in 12 minutes	_____
Weight trained for 30 minutes	_____
Played softball for I hour	_____
Played basketball for I hour	_____
Golfed 9 holes	_____

Nutritional Questions

Record all food and drink for a 24-hour period. Input your record into the computer and print out an analysis.

Record one meal (breakfast, lunch, or dinner) and analyze for calories.

How many calories of fat _____ carbohydrates _____ protein _____

Analyze the following meal for calories:
    I Big Mac
    I large order of french fries
    1 12-ounce coke
How many calories of fat _____ carbohydrates _____ protein _____

Analyze the following foods for calories.
    3 glazed donuts
Simple carbohydrates _____ complex carbohydrates _____ fat _____ protein _____

Snack of 12-ounce coke, bag of peanuts, bag of chips, Snickers candy bar
Simple carbohydrates _____ complex carbohydrates _____ fat _____ protein _____

8 ounces milk, spaghetti, I cup of green beans, baked potato, tossed green salad
Simple carbohydrates _____ complex carbohydrates _____ fat _____ protein _____

Blood Pressure

Use a sphygmomanometer or an automatic blood pressure system to determine the blood pressure of each student. An automated computer software program such as *DynaPulse* will take the blood pressure and provide the students with an informative print-out. Using a reference chart or a computer software program, have each student determine a blood pressure rating based on age and gender.

Anatomy And Physiology

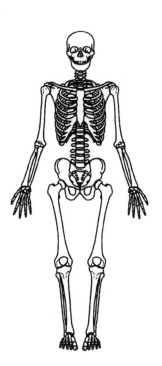

There are several inexpensive anatomy and physiology computer software programs available on the market. Examples of some programs are *Bodyworks, 3-D body Adventure, and ADAM.* Ways to integrate these programs into a physical activity setting include:

- ✎ Analyze what muscles were used during a workout. Find the muscles in the software program.
- ✎ Using a software program, follow the flow of blood through the heart as you exercise.
- ✎ Using a software program, determine what role the nervous system plays in exercise.

Exercise Equipment

Exercise Bike

When using an exercise bike, a student should adjust the seat height so that when the pedal is in the lowest position, the leg is almost straight. Turn on the computerized LCD display and set the timer for five minutes. Push the start button. Have the students alternate the display between speed, distance, and pedal RPM as they pedal.

1. Record the heart rate at 1 minute _____, 3 minutes _____, and 5 minutes _____.
2. Record the total distance biked _____.

Stair Climber

Select the program and difficulty level. Select the work-out time, press start and adjust speed. Periodically check the distance climbed in feet or floors, energy expended in METS or calories, time remaining, or climbing speed in feet/minutes.

1. Exercise for two minutes at each of the program modes and record the information.

Program Mode	Difficulty Level	Heart Rate	Distance	Calories

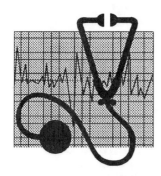

Heart Rate Monitors

During physical education class, have all the students wear heart rate monitors. If there are not enough heart rate monitors for each student, the students may alternate wearing the monitors for 10 -15 minutes or rotate the use of the monitors on a daily basis.

Before utilizing a heart rate monitor the student should determine his/her aerobic target zone. With the monitor in place, have the students lie down on the floor and remain quiet for about 2 minutes. This will provide a rough estimate of the resting heart rate.

As the students begin exercising, have them periodically check their heart rate. Explain to them what should be occurring with their heart rate. This will give them information on their exercise intensity.

If a heart rate monitor with memory is available (e.g., *Polar Vantage XL),* a print-out of the heart rate can be produced. The print-out will give the teacher and students the percentage of time spent in, above, and below the aerobic target zone. This information can be very valuable to both the teacher and student in evaluating the physical education activity program.

Physical Fitness Testing

Have the students input the raw scores for their physical fitness tests into a computer software program. After inputting the data, the students can print-out their scores and ratings. This information can be very beneficial in establishing fitness goals. Software programs such as *Fitness Testing, Fitness Analyst, and Fitnessgram* can be used.

TEST	SCORE	RATING
Cardiovascular	_____	_____
Muscular strength	_____	_____
Muscular endurance	_____	_____
Flexibility	_____	_____
Body composition	_____	_____

Further Information

Information on the technological equipment and computer software programs listed in this article can be obtained by contacting the sources listed. As technological equipment and computer software is constantly changing, it is suggested you contact the source and receive the latest information on their product.

SOURCES		
Skyndex	Country Technology	608-735-4718
Dine Healthy	Dine Systems	716-688-2400
Fitness testing software	Mark Stanbrough-ESU	316-342-7253
Fitnessgram	Cooper Institute	214-701-8001
Heart monitors	Polar	800-227-1314
Body Composition	Futrex	301-670-1106
Dynapulse	Pulse Metric	619-546-9461
Bodyworks	Softkey International	617-494-1200
3-D Body Adventure	Knowledge Adventure	818-542-4200
ADAM	ADAM Software	404-953-ADAM
Nutritionist	N-Squared Computing	503-364-9118
Food Processor	ESHA Research	503-585-6242
Fitness Analyst	Brittingham Software	908-879-4991

IDEAS III:

Section Two

Individual Activities

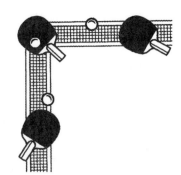

FLOOR PONG

By Michelle DiLisio
Chanute High School
Chanute, KS

National Standards

✎ Demonstrates competency in many movement forms and proficiency in a few movement forms.
✎ Understands that physical activity provides the opportunity for enjoyment, challenge, self-expression, and social interaction.

Introductions

If you are seeking an activity that is inexpensive, maximizes participation, and is easy to learn, then floor pong is the game to begin at your school. The game is great for improving students' agility and coordination. Floor Pong tends to equalize differences in age, gender, strength, and athletic ability.

Basic Rules for Floor Pong

Floor Pong is a combination of tennis and table tennis. It can be played by two or four people. The court dimensions are 8 feet wide by 30 feet long. The net is an 8'X 18" piece of plywood. Regular ping pong paddles and balls are used in this game. A game consists of scoring 21 points. Service changes every 5 points. If the score reaches 20-20 (deuce), service alternates with each point, and a player or team must attain a 2 point advantage to win. Doubles rules are similar to singles, but partners must alternate in returning opponents' shots. For serves, the ball must be bounced and then hit directly over the net, after which all returns are made after the first bounce. No smashes allowed.

Gymnasium floors are easily converted Floor Pong courts. Many times existing lines are quite usable and it is possible to set your courts up so that they share sidelines. We use the volleyball sidelines as our baseline and run 10-12 courts right down the center of the gym, with an additional 2-4 courts possible around the outside perimeter of the volleyball court. This makes it very easy to accommodate 12-16 singles matches (24-32 students). Regular folding mats also work well as make-shift nets.

Lead-up Activities for Floor Pong

King/Queen of the Court

This is a progressive work-up game in which players play one point matches. The goal of the game is to work one's way to the king's court and remain in this court by beating challengers. Equipment needed for this game includes a paddle for each player and one ball for each court.

Rules: The rotation to use when playing this game is illustrated below. At the beginning of the game, place two players on each court. Designate one court as the King's Court. All winners will move toward this court. Losers on all courts except the King's Court will remain and serve the next point. Winners on the King's Court will remain and serve the next point. Losers on the King's Court will go to the end of the line at the beginning of the rotation.

King's Court

King's Court	Team B	Team D	Team F	Team H	Winners move up to the next court. Losers stay and serve. If a team in King's Court loses, they go to open side on Court #5.
Team A	Team C	Team E	Team G	Team I	
Court 1	Court 2	Court 3	Court 4	Court 5	

← **Winners move in this direction**

34

Around the World

The class is divided into two equal teams, on each side of the net. The groups should line up one behind the other on opposite baselines. The first person in one line drop-hits the ball to the first person on the other side of the net. After hitting the ball, the person must run around the court past the right net post to the end of the line at the other side of the court. The goal of the class should be to hit as many consecutive balls in a row as possible. The group should be encouraged to work together toward a common goal.

Around the World

Ball . . . . ▶

Run ⟶

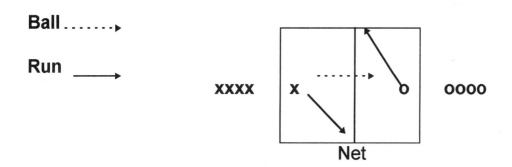

XXXX X   O OOOO

Net

Four Way Rapid-Fire

Four Way Rapid-Fire

Player B serves to Player A, C, or D. Player B immediately moves off the court to the end of the line behind Player Q, while Player 0 takes Player B's place on the court. Play continues, with a player on any court immediately replaced by the next player in the line after the ball has been played in that court.

GFE   RST

D	C
B	A

QPO   LMN

Scoring: There are two possible ways to score in this lead-up activity. The students can play for a specified time, keeping individual scores. The player losing the fewest points wins the game. The second way to score this activity is to have all students on the same court be a team. Keep a team score. Team with the fewest points wins the game.

Conclusion

Floor Pong is an inexpensive activity that can be easily added to any physical education curriculum. It is an excellent activity to include as a novel activity in a racket sports unit. The activities that can be played with Floor Pong are also excellent fitness and conditioning games.

Orienteering
A Challenging Adventure
Unit for
Middle School Students

By Paul W. Darst
Arizona State University
Tempe, AZ
Don P. Hicks
Fort Worth Day School
Fort Worth, TX

National Standards

- Applies movement concepts and principles to the learning and development of motor skills. Achieves and maintains a health-enhancing level of physical fitness.
- Demonstrates responsible personal and social behavior in physical activity settings.
- Understands that physical activity provides the opportunity for enjoyment, challenge, self-expression, and social interaction.

Introduction

Orienteering is an activity that combines cross-country running/walking with map reading and compass skills. It is a lifetime activity that enhances an individual's cardiovascular endurance. It is often referred to as the "thinking sport" or "smart running." It is a good activity for coed classes and, by its nature, creates teamwork at the middle school level. Most middle school students are not familiar With the sport of orienteering, thus its novelty is highly motivating.

Orienteering activities can easily be adapted to the available facilities of most middle schools. Learning activities can be modified and adapted for use in a classroom, gymnasium, or outdoors. Compasses and xeroxed maps of the school grounds can be used to develop an exciting unit of instruction. A nearby park or vacant outdoor area can be used to set up challenging orienteering courses.

The following teaching sequence of activities has been field-tested with middle school students and has been shown to be educationally sound and effective in developing orienteering skills.

Orienteering Activities

1. **_Parts of the compass_**. Before students can do any orienteering, they will need to know the six basic parts of a compass. These parts are listed below.

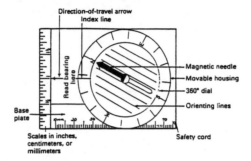

2. **_Knowledge assessment_**. A simple test to use to assess the students' knowledge of compass directions and degrees is illustrated below.

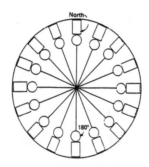

3. **_Finding a direction_**.   The next step is to help students determine the to go if they are given a bearing (e.g., 200°). With the students holding the compass properly, have there set 200° by moving the compass housing until 200 meets the line-of-direction arrow on the base plate. Once the bearing is set, the students will rotate their body (in place) until the magnetic north needle falls directly over the orienting arrow.

4. **_Determining a bearing_**. Another way to use the compass is to have students face various visible landmarks. Students then "shoot a bearing" from where they are standing to the landmark. As they face the object, they turn the compass housing until the magnetic north needle falls directly over the orienting arrow. They will read the bearing they are heading where the compass housing meets the line of direction arrow.

5. **_Forming a triangle_**. In order to practice walking and moving with a compass, students should place an object (e.g., penny, bean bag, cone marker) on the ground between their feet. Each student should select a bearing less than 90°. The students should then find the bearing and walk 10 paces in that direction (Pace = 2 steps). Next, add 120° to the original bearing and walk 10 paces in the direction of the new bearing. Finally, they should add 120° to the last bearing and walk 10 paces in the direction of the third bearing. At this point, the students should be back where they started. Variation of this activity is to form a square instead of a triangle. Follow all of the same procedures except add 90° instead of 120° and form a four-sided, rather than three-sided object.

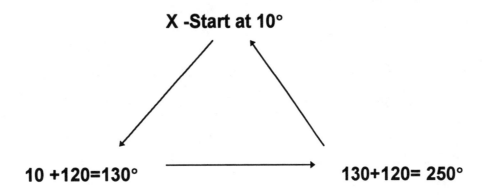

X -Start at 10°

10 +120=130°   **130+120= 250°**

6. **_Numbers and numerals_**. Before class, tape numbers 1 -10 (or more) on the floor in a scattered manner. Roman numerals I-X (or more) should be taped to the gym walls. The students stand on any number and shoot a bearing to the corresponding roman numeral on a wall. Record the bearing and move to the next highest number. It is a good idea to limit the number of students who may be at any given number on the floor at the same time.

7. **_Forming a Christmas tree_.** This is a good activity to use for a cool-down or when space is limited. The students place a dot in the southwest quadrant on a piece of graph paper. From this point, have the students draw lines following the bearings and distances listed below. By the end of the activity a formation similar to a Christmas tree should be formed.

Bearing	Distance (cm)	Bearing	Distance (cm)
1. 269	2.2	9. 136	6.3
2. 2	2.7	10. 293	1.9
3. 266	4.9	11. 141	5.2
4. 30	6.5	12. 284	2.4
5. 246	2.6	13. 125	5.2
6. 34	5.0	14. 271	5.1
7. 244	2.0	15. 179	2.7
8. 37	4.6		

8. **_Map work_.** Students learn how to determine the degree bearings between points on a map. The teacher marks a number of points on a map. Copies of the map are given to students. They are instructed to find the bearing and distance between the points. For example, if 10 numbered points are marked on the map, students find the bearing and distance from #1 to # 2 #2 to #3, etc.

9. **_Destination unknown_.** Divide the class into four equal teams. Each team is given a card with the bearings and paces as listed below. All four teams start from the same starting point and they should all end up at the same destination.

Team 1	Team 2	Team 3	Team 4
90 d/l00 p	360 d/l00 p	45 d/71 p	315 d/71 p
360 d/l00 p	90 d/l00 p	315 d/71 p	45 d/71 p
270 d/l00 p	360 d/l00 p	45 d/71 p	315 d/71 p
360 d/100 p	270 d/l00 p	315 d/71 p	45 d/71 p

10. **_Cross-country or point-to-point orienteering_.** Ten or more checkpoints listed are listed on five or six master maps. Each student is given a map of the school grounds showing landmarks. At the start of this activity, each student must go to a master map and copy the

checkpoints on his/her map. The teacher starts the stopwatch when the students are handed their maps (the time it takes to copy the checkpoints on their map is part of their total time). A code word or symbol is located at each checkpoint. When the students have visited all checkpoints and recorded all code words, they must race back to the finish line and record the time it took to complete the course. The student with the lowest time is the winner. (Note: to ensure that all students visit each checkpoint, a different stamp or colored pencil should be used at each checkpoint). A system of adding a certain amount of time to the student's score for each incorrect code word/symbol should be used in determining the winner.

11. ***Variation of point-to-point orienteering***. The checkpoints are marked on the master maps, but are not numbered. Also listed on the master maps next to each checkpoint are the names of three to four students. The checkpoint with their name is the checkpoint they must visit first. At that point, they will find an information card with the bearing and paces to the next checkpoint. After the starting signal, the students copy the checkpoints on their maps and then travel to the point where their names are listed. Upon arriving, they record the number of the checkpoint and the code word/symbol for the point on their scorecard. The students shoot a bearing and jog the number of paces in that direction in pursuit of the next checkpoint. The students record the code word/symbol at each checkpoint.

12. ***Score orienteering***. In this competitive activity, the various checkpoints have different point values. The checkpoints that are the furthest away and the most difficult to locate are given the highest point values. The object is to secure the most points within a given time limit. Students begin by copying the checkpoints from a master map onto their own maps of the school grounds. Once the starting signal is given, students must visit as many checkpoints as possible within a given time limit. Students who are late returning to the finish line can be assessed a penalty (point deduction) or disqualified. Each student will need a score card to record the clue at each checkpoint.

13. **_Descriptive orienteering_**. This activity requires a compass and pacing skills, b no map. Students find the check points as fast as possible by following a bearin a distance, and a descriptive clue word(s). Each student is given a sheet similar the one shown below.

Descriptive Orienteering Sheet

Checkpoint	Bearing	Description	Distance	Clue
1	90°	Irrigation Ditch	50 yards	
2	180°	Cement Court	100 meters	
3	230 °	Soccer Goal	200 feet	
4	160°	Dumpster	35 feet	
5	341°	Pitcher's Mound	75 meters	
6	45°	High Jump Pit	400 feet	
7	106°	Batting Cage	150 yards	
8	270°	Palm Tree	250 meters	
9	83°	Horizontal Bars	350 feet	
10	200°	Power Pole	80 yards	

All the students begin at a designated starting point and return to that point before they start to the next point. Each checkpoint has a letter, word, or team name that must be recorded in the "Clue" column. The teacher is stationed at the starting point to monitor student progress throughout the competition. A variation of this activity includes challenging students by giving them only the respective bearings and distances to the various checkpoints. When a checkpoint is found, the bearing and distance for the next checkpoint will be given. It is recommended that students be assigned different starting checkpoints for this activity.

Conclusion

Orienteering is a fun and novel way to improve students' fitness levels. As students develop skills and begin to work in groups, this "thinking sport" can be an excellent way to improve the social skills (teamwork, cooperation, and group cohesion) of middle school students.

References
Pangrazi, R., and Darst, P. (1991). *Dynamic Physical Education for Secondary School Students - Curriculum and Instruction*. 2nd Edition. MacMillan Publishing Co. New York, NY.

KITES

By Michelle DiLisio
Chanute High School
Chanute, KS

National Standards

✎ Understands that physical activity provides the opportunity for enjoyment, challenge, self-expression, and social interaction.

Introduction

Kite flying is an engaging activity for students of all ages. All that is needed is a kite, a light breeze, good weather, and an open space. This is an excellent activity to include in a physical education program as the darkness and cold of winter give way to the warm breezes of spring.

As most students have not had much experience in building a kite, the teacher has a rare opportunity to begin with a group of students having similar abilities. Almost anyone can follow the kite-building directions. Those students who have difficulty understanding the directions can ask for tips and assistance from other students. The amount of time used in a kite unit may vary, depending on the objectives. Successful units may be as short as three or four days. Objectives may include terminology, history, safety tips, launching and landing, and problems with flight and their cures. This is also a good unit to work with cross-curricular instruction (math, science, writing, etc.)

Some additional benefits of this unit include cooperation, recognition, and challenge. The students help and support each other in this activity and share in each others' success. Recognition is given to some students who may not normally excel in traditional physical education activities. All students have the opportunity to experience the satisfaction of achievement through patience and concentration. Many students have commented favorably on this unit and several students asked about new kite designs for future units.

Kite design and kite building are two activities that can lead to some exciting experiences. Designing, building, and flying kites can lead to many contests within your classes. Awards for the highest flying, longest tail, best crash-and-burn, and the prettiest kite are just a few suggestions for various contests you might wish to conduct.

The kite designs suggested in this article are simple to make, inexpensive, and fly well. The main emphasis in this unit is recreational FUN and a hope the students will share this activity with their families.

Basic Kite Terminology and Safety Guidelines

Before the students begin to build their kites, make sure they understand the terms and safety guidelines associated with kite design.

Term	Definition
Line	String used to fly kites; holds kite into wind and is the control device.
Launch	To get kite "up" and flying.
Drift	Allow kite to float in the wind, letting out string as the kite drifts.
Snubbing	As kite is allowed to drift, the line is gradually slowed down to a halt.
Landing	Getting a kite down from flight.
Power loop	A strong thrust of the kite in a big circle, gradually descending with each successive "loop".
Walked down	Bringing the kite down by anchoring the line to a solid object (tree) and walking toward the kite while letting the line slide under the hand.
Lift	The angle of the kite and kite construction allows the kite to be "lifted" up into the air.
Drag	A decrease in air movement on the backside of the kite which causes a condition called "drag". The weight of the kite also causes a portion of the drag.
Bridle	The lines attached to the kite from the main line; form a tow point.
Vent	A section either cut out of a kite or built into a kite, which helps stabilize it during flight.
Oscillation	A sideward "wobble" of a kite in flight. This wobble indicates a need for venting.
Tow point	Point at which the flying line is connected to the bridle or kite and sets at the correct angle to the wind. Varies according to wind conditions.
Spine	Backbone of the kite which helps hold it taut where necessary.
Struts	Side and cross members that stretch and support the kite frame.
Tails	Added to the bottom of a kite to add drag, but not weight. A good tail should act as a stabilizer.
Sail	Main body, or cover, of the kite.

Safety tips:

- ➘ Only fly in open space, away from buildings, trees, people.
- ➘ Never fly where there are overhead electrical lines or telephone wires.
- ➘ Never fly within 5 miles of an airport. A federal regulation prohibits it.
- ➘ When walking a kite, be sure to look where you are going.

Kite Designs

Sled Kite

Materials - One piece of plastic; Two -28 1/21 x 3116" dowels; strapping tape; 85 1/2" flying line for bridle

Instructions - Using the drawing and a marking pen, draw and cut kite sail the from plastic. Open sail and lay flat. Tape dowels between A and B on both sides of sail, placing tape under plastic and folding it up and over dowel and to plastic. Tape dowels to plastic near center of each dowel. Reinforce bridle points (C) on each wing with tape. Fold sail and match points C. Using paper or leather punch make a hole through the tape on both wings at once. Tie bridle through holes. Find center of bridle. Tie a loop at midpoint. Attach flying line to loop. Dowels should be on the outside (sky side) when flying. A tail may be added at the bottom of each strut for flying in stronger winds.

Delta Moth Kite

Materials: One piece of plastic; 1/4" dowels in the following lengths: one 22 ½", two 21", one cross strut approximately 18 ½"; two 1 ½" x ¼" pieces of plastic tubing; strapping tape

Instructions - Using the drawing, draw and cut sail from plastic. Keep kite folded at center fold; fold back one wing at A-B. Tape wings along fold to form keel. Reinforce nose of keel with tape. Insert 22 1/2" dowel for spine. Close tail of keel with tape. Reinforce tow point with tape. Punch hole for tow point. Fold tubing in half. Cut off one corner at fold. Slide tubing onto 21 " side struts with open ends of tubing 14" from ends of dowels. Place side struts on wings of kite with one end at C and tape at C, D, and just below tubing. Fit cross strut dowel into one side strut and cut to fit into second strut. Insert into side struts. Attach flying line at tow point. A tail may be added for flying in stronger winds. Cut strips from plastic and tie together for an inexpensive tail.

Vented Box Kite

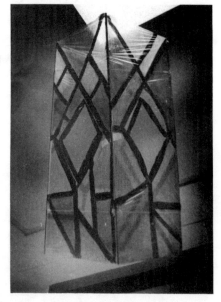

Materials: One trash bag; six 36" x ¼ " dowels; Eight pieces of plastic tubing, one ½" x ¼" ; strapping tape

Instructions: Cut off closed bottom of bag. Fold bag in half lengthwise. Mark and snip each end at fold. Fold bag in half lengthwise again. Fold bag in half crosswise with ends meeting. Cut a 4 x 6 inch triangle for one folded corner through all layers. Unfold bag. Fold tubing piece in half. Cut off one folded corner. Repeat for remaining seven pieces. Measure the length of the trash bag and cut four dowels to the same length. Slide two pieces of tubing onto each of four dowels for side struts, placing open ends of tubing six inches from ends of dowels. Tape side struts to inside of kite at side seams and between marks of the first fold. Cut remaining dowels to make four cross struts approximately 19 ¾ inches long. You may need to adjust the length slightly. Fit cross struts into tubing, diagonally across the inside, two at each end. Mark a tow point one inch from top of kite at one side strut. Reinforce with tape. Punch hole. Tie flying line.

Tetrahedron Kite

Materials: 24 straws per kite, kite string, tissue paper (one sheet per kite), rubber cement, scissors

Instructions

A. Assembling one tetrahedron

1. Measure one piece of string about one meter in length. Put three straws on the meter string and tie them into a triangle.
2. Measure and cut two pieces of string about 35 cm long. Tie each of the short strings to a corner of the triangle.
3. Slip a straw onto each string and tie together tightly to form a rhombus.
4. Slip a third straw onto one of the loose ends of a string.
5. Tie the end of the string to the vortex of the triangle that has nothing tied to it yet. This completes the first tetrahedron.
6. Repeat this procedure to complete three more tetrahedrons.

B. Cutting the tissue coverings

The sections that make up the covering of the kite can all be cut from one sheet of tissue paper. Plastic trash bags also work well as the covering of this kite.

1. Cut out the pattern.
2. Fold a full sheet of tissue paper in half, neatly, then in fourths, and then again in eighths.
3. Lay the pattern on the folded tissue paper and cut the tissue with scissors all around the pattern except along the fold. DO NOT CUT ALONG THE FOLD.
4. Unfold the tissue.

C. Mounting the tissue paper.
1. Put a small amount of glue along the fold in the center of the tissue paper. Lay any one straw in the center along the fold. The trick is to put the straw exactly in the crease of the tissue paper.
2. Cover both of the tissue paper flaps lying outside the straw triangle with glue. Fold these flaps over the straws and glue them down inside the triangle. Be careful to smooth all creases and bumps from the outside surface.
3. Flip the tetrahedron so that the opposite side comes down on the other side of the tissue pattern. Glue the flap as before.
4. Repeat this procedure for the other three tetrahedrons.

D. Assembling the kite
1. Tie three of the tetrahedrons in a triangle to form the base. Be sure all of the tetrahedrons are facing the same way.
2. Place and tie the fourth tetrahedron above the triangle formed by the first three. Be sure all of the tetrahedrons are facing the same way. If necessary, extra string may be added.

E. Let's go fly a kite
1. Cut off all left over string.
2. For flying, make a Y-shaped harness by tying the string from the tip of the top tetrahedron to the bottom tetrahedron. The outside surface of the tissue covering the tetrahedron should face the wind. It may be necessary to tie a tail to the bottom of the Y-shaped harness if the wind is too strong.

Source: Let's Go Fly A Kite by Anita Baranczuk and Jane Grey B. Browning. KAMLE Symposium, February 18, 1994.

SLED KITE

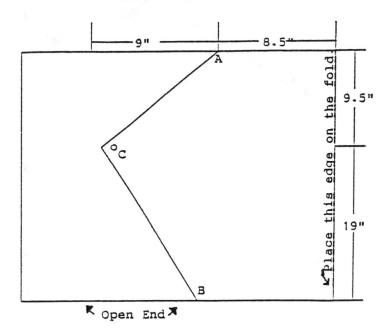

9"

8.5"

A

Place this edge on the fold

9.5"

19"

°C

B

↖ Open End ↗

DELTA MOTH

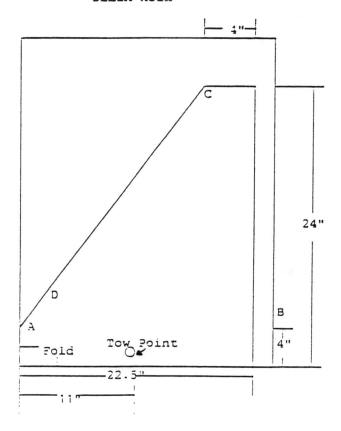

4"

C

24"

D

B

A

4"

Fold

Tow Point

22.5"

11"

49

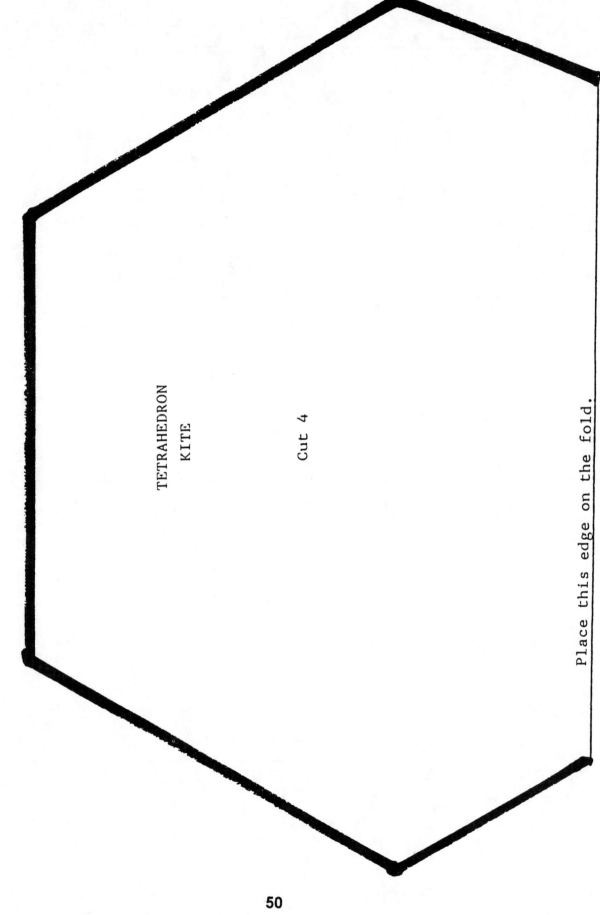

TETRAHEDRON
KITE

Cut 4

Place this edge on the fold.

50

Bouldering Walls

By Jeff McAdoo
Quail Run Elementary
Lawrence, KS

National Standards

- Demonstrates competency in many movement forms and proficiency in a few movement forms.
- Achieves and maintains a health-enhancing level of physical fitness.
- Demonstrates responsible personal and social behavior in physical activity settings.
- Understands that physical activity provides the opportunity for enjoyment, challenge, self-expression, and social interaction.

Introduction

Indoor rock climbing, or sport climbing, is a rapidly growing physical activity. Climbing gyms can be found in most cities throughout the country. Many physical educators who have experienced the benefits of this activity have built climbing walls in their gyms. One concern which may make physical educators reticent to add this activity program to their program is safety. Since very few teachers are familiar with ropes and technical gear needed to rock climb, they view climbing as an activity that could produce many injuries.

An alternative form of rock climbing called "bouldering" is a safe way for the non-climbing teacher to include climbing in the physical education curriculum. Bouldering walls are not more than 10 feet high. The participants climb across, rather than up, the walls. No technical gear is needed since their feet never go more than three to four feet off the floor. By constructing bouldering walls that have various angles and caves, a simple bouldering wall can become a sufficient training area for all but the most highly trained climbers.

Basic construction of the walls consists of ¾" plywood screwed into a 2 x 4 wooden frame using standard construction techniques. Half-inch holes are drilled randomly in the plywood (30 or more per 4' x 8' sheet of plywood), and 3/8" T-nuts (available at most hardware stores) are placed in the holes from the back side of the wall. The artificial rocks, called "holds" are screwed into these holds wherever the teacher decides to place them. Smaller holds that do not protrude as much from the wall on the lower areas are used as foot holds. In the event a climber slides down the wall, there will be less chance of injury. The bouldering walls can be attached to the gym walls in a variety of ways. More specific instructions are available through climbing manufacturers or by visiting a climbing gym.

Safety Guidelines

Once the walls have been installed, the students need to use the walls in a safe manner. The basic safety rules include:

- Always place mats below the climbing area.
- The students should practice jumping backward off the wall from progressively higher heights. They should only climb as high as they can comfortably jump off the wall.
- Students should not stand on the mats behind a climber. Make sure the climber has a clear landing area.
- Students should be instructed to jump off the wall when they start to fall and not to fight to stay on the wall. This technique enables them to dismount under control.
- Do not allow any horseplay on the wall.
- Students should not touch a student while he/she is climbing.
- Students should understand that climbing a bouldering wall does not prepare them for outside rock climbing.

Activities on Bouldering Walls

Routes and Bouldering Games

With time and practice, basic climbing will become too easy for many students. At that time, climbing routes can be designed. To create climbing routes, use various colors of tape (red, blue, green) to mark the way in which the student needs to climb the wall. In addition to determining direction, students should be told which holds they can and cannot use on that route.

Sit Down Starts

The wall will seem much larger if the students start their climbs from a sifting position. Students should start with their hands and feet on the wall and buttocks on the mat. They are not allowed to touch the mat with their hands and feet once they are on the wall. Climbing holds may need to lowered on the wall.

Stretch

With the students in pairs, one student climbs on the wall and finds a "hold" for his/her base. The student must remain in contact with the base (using any part of his/her body) and touch as many rocks as possible without falling. The climber's partner counts the number of rocks that are touched by the climber.

Stick Game

With the students in pairs, one student climbs on the wall. The partner uses a stick (hockey stick, yardstick, etc.), to point to a rock that the climber must touch and indicates the body part to be used to touch it.

Bleacher Climbing

If you have the type of bleachers that fold back against the wall, you can use these bleachers to determine if your students would enjoy bouldering. Instruct the students to use the spaces between the boards for hand and foot holds. Have them move across the face of the "wall" to a designated point.

Conclusion

Bouldering is an excellent activity to add to your physical education program. If you are interested in adding this to your curriculum, visit a climbing gym in your area. Most of these gyms will have bouldering walls as well as vertical walls. Further information can also be found in climbing magazines such as _Rock and Ice_.

IDEAS III:

Section Three

Team Activities

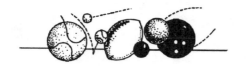

Lead-up Activities for Skill and Fitness

By Sandy Meneley
Landon Middle School
Topeka, KS

National Standards

- Demonstrates competency in many movement forms and proficiency in a few movement forms.
- Exhibits a physically active lifestyle.
- Demonstrates responsible personal and social behavior in physical activity settings.

Introduction

Often, students at the middle school level are not motivated to work on their motor skills through the use of drills. However, as soon as they are placed into a game-like setting, their motivation and focus improve. If a teacher can design lead-up games that focus on one or two skills, the students will be placed in a situation where they can get needed practice in an enjoyable environment. The lead-up games presented below can be used in basketball, floor hockey, and volleyball to improve students' skill and level of fitness in a motivating environment.

Basketball

Aerial Basketball. This game is played like regular basketball with the following modifications.

- No guarding the person with the ball.
- No jump shots are allowed.
- No one can strip the ball from the player with the ball.
- The ball may be advanced down the court by passing only.
- After playing this game for a period of time, allow the person with the ball three dribbles. The students would have the option of dribbling three times, passing, or shooting.

Bowling Pin Call the Shot. Place a bowling pin in the center of the gym. Students should be divided into groups of four. The object of the game is to score points by knocking over a bowling pin and shooting different types of shots at a basket. The rules are:

↳ The first person in each line rolls a basketball at the bowling pin. If the pin is missed, the player runs and retrieves the ball and gives it to the next person in the line. The next person in that line tries to knock the pin over.

↳ This process continues until someone on one of the teams knocks the pin over. This team scores one point.

↳ After the pin is knocked over, every team member runs to an assigned basket and shoots for one minute using a designated type of shot (lay-up, free throw, 3 point, jump shot).

↳ Each team keeps a total of the number of shots they make (one point for each made shot).

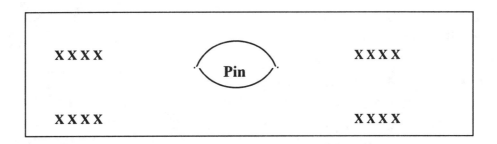

Addition 21. The object of the game is to be the first group to score 21 points. The following rules are used:

- Divide the students into groups of four to five students. Each team is assigned to a basket.
- The first person on each team shoots a free throw (two points if the shot is made). If the shot is not made, the next person in the line shoots. If the shot is made, the person can the shoot a lay-up (one point if the shot is made). Whether the lay-up is made or missed, the next person in line shoots.
- This process continues until a team reaches 21 points.
- A modification to this game is to have the first person shoot a free throw and if the person makes the shot, he/she continues to shoot until that person misses. After a miss, the person still gets a chance to shoot a lay-up.

Floor Hockey

Score It Up Hockey. The object of the game is to score as many goals as possible in a two-minute period. Students should be organized in groups of three and arranged as indicated below. The rules of the game include:

- The game is started with a face off between the offensive and defensive lines.
- Defensive players are trying to keep the offensive players from scoring a goal. They can do this by intercepting or stealing the puck and dribbling back to half court. Once back at half-court, a new face off begins.
- Offensive players are attempting to score goals. They can do this by sending the puck across the end line. Once a goal is scored, a new face off begins.
- Goalies are trying to stop the puck and may not leave the goalie area. They may stop the puck with their stick or their feet.

- Sideline players do not have hockey sticks but they may use their feet to keep the puck in play. They may not score and need to immediately send the puck back into the field of play.
- Rotate the lines every two minutes.

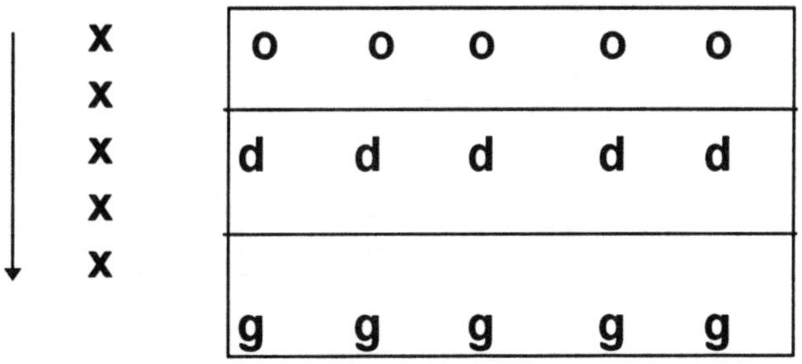
x
x
x
x
x
o o o o o
d d d d d
g g g g g

Volleyball

<u>Shower Service Ball</u>. The object of this game is for a team to serve volleyballs over a net without the opposite team catching the serve before it hits the ground. The basic guidelines of this game follow:

- Divide the students into two teams (more if court space allows). The teams should be in scattered formation on opposite sides of the volleyball court.
- To begin the game, one team is given two volleyballs. Anyone from that team can serve, but the serve must occur anywhere behind the volleyball endline.
- If the serve clears the net, the opposite team must catch it, run behind their endline and immediately serve it back to the other team. If this team fails to catch it, then the serving team gets a point. If the serve fails to clear the net, the receiving team gets a point.
- After a certain amount of time, start adding volleyballs and continue to add as many volleyballs as safety allows.

Team Handball

Choose Your Score. The object of the game is to move the ball down the court and score in one of the following ways:

1. Throw a ball at the wall - 1 point.
2. Knock a ball off a cone which is placed on the baseline - 2 points.
3. Shoot a basket outside the free throw lane - 3 points.
4. Shoot a three point basket - 4 points.

The basic team handball rules are followed except for the following modifications:

⇨ Once a player has the ball in his/her possession, that person may not be guarded or have the ball taken away.
⇨ No dribbling or running with the ball is allowed.
⇨ The only way to advance the ball down the court is to pass it to a teammate.
⇨ After a score, the ball is given to the goalie and play resumes from that point.
⇨ Play the game with two goalies.
⇨ Scoring options should be included gradually during the unit. For example, on day one, the students may only score using the wall as a goal. On day two, they have two choices: the wall or knocking the ball off the cone.

Conclusion

Middle school students are motivated when they are involved in a game-like activity. When designing lead-up games, a teacher should limit the skills that can be utilized in the game, create more scoring options, and maximize participation. Carefully designed lead-up games can be an extremely useful way to develop students' basic skills in any sport.

Fitball Football

By Sue Tillery
Rockwood Valley Middle School
Manchester, MO

National Standards

✎ Demonstrates competency in many movement forms and proficiency in a few movement forms.
✎ Demonstrates understanding and respect for differences among people in physical activity
✎ settings.
✎ Understands that physical activity provides the opportunity for enjoyment, challenge, self-expression, and social interaction.

Introduction

At the middle school level, either your students know a great deal about the game of football or they know very little. Often, the basic skills your students possess fall into similar categories: the students either have very good fundamental skills or they have poor skills. As a teacher, it is difficult to create lead-up games that equalize these differences. The lead-up games listed below develop basic skills, challenge all students, and maximize fitness benefits.

Flag Football Tag

Divide the class into two groups and give different colored flag football belts to each team. The object of the game is for players to successfully carry footballs from one goal line to the other goal line without having their flags pulled.

To start the game, one team (offense) lines up on the goal line. Each person on this team should have a football. The defense stands anywhere they want in the middle of the field. On a signal, the offensive team starts to run toward the other goal line. If a person with a football gets his/her flag pulled, that person puts the ball on the ground and walks or jogs to the goal line. Persons who successfully carry the football across the goal line without their flags being pulled score one point for their team. Switch offense and defense at the end of each run.

Surprise Football

Divide the class into two teams. If the class is large (30+) divide into four teams. The object of the game is to get the "treasure" from one goal line to other without having the person with the "treasure" getting tagged.

The team on offense is given two objects; a coin (treasure) and a black chip (bomb). To start the game, the offense huddles and gives the treasure and bomb to two of the players on their team. The offense breaks the huddle and lines up anywhere along the goal line. All team members should have their hand clasped, as if they had the treasure or the bomb. The defense can be anywhere in the middle of the playing field. On a signal, the offensive team attempts to run to the opposite goal line. If a player is tagged by a defensive players, he/she must stop and open both hands to show whether he/she is carrying the treasure or the bomb.

The offense scores seven points if the person carrying the treasure is able to cross the goal line without getting tagged. If the defense tags the person with the bomb, the defensive team loses three points. Switch the offense and defense after each run.

Football 21

Divide the class into teams of five or six students. The offensive team consists of a quarterback and receivers. The defensive team consists of pass defenders and one pass rusher. The pass rusher must slow count to three before he/she can rush the quarterback.

The object of the game is to be the first team to score exactly 21 points. In order to score points, a pass must be completed. The point value of the pass is dependent upon the place at which the pass is caught. An incomplete pass is worth zero points.

Start the game with a center snap to the quarterback. The pass receivers run out into the scoring area. The quarterback can pass to any of his/her receivers. After each pass, the offensive and defensive teams switch places. Each time a team returns to the offensive or defensive role, all team members must assume a different role; e.g., quarterback must become a receiver, pass rusher must become pass defender.

A team must score exactly 21 points. If a team has 20 points and the next pass is caught in the two point area, the team loses all points and starts at zero.

	1 pt.	2 pt.	3 pt.
QB		PR PD	
	PR PD		PR PD

QB=Quarterback
PR=Pass Receiver
PD=Pass Defender

Aerobic Football

This game is a cross between football and ultimate frisbee. Divide the class into two equal teams. The basic rules include:

⇨ Play is started with a center snap from the middle of the field.
⇨ The offense can pass, hand-off, or run with the ball.
⇨ The ball may only be held for three seconds before giving the ball to another teammate.
⇨ In order to score a touchdown, the ball must be passed and caught behind the goal line. The ball cannot be run across the goal line.
⇨ The defense can steal the ball any time the ball is in the air. They may not attempt to knock or rip the ball from another player's arms.
⇨ The defense can stop a player who is running with the ball by tagging that person.
⇨ If the ball goes out of bounds, the last team to touch the ball puts the ball back in play with a center snap from that point.
⇨ If the ball is dropped, the first team to get to the ball has possession.
⇨ A touchdown is worth six points. The team scored against should immediately pick up the football and start on offense. Do not bring the ball back to the center after each touchdown.

Conclusion

The traditional game of football does not encourage the development of fitness and, often, is very difficult to play at the middle school level. By simplifying the rules, limiting the skills used, and maximizing participation, middle school students will discover that football can become one of their favorite units.

Hockey for the Middle School

By Paul Darst and Belinda Stillwell
Arizona State University
Tempe, AZ

National Standards

✍ Demonstrates competency in many movement forms and proficiency in a few movement forms.
✍ Achieves and maintains a health-enhancing level of physical fitness.
✍ Understands that physical activity provides the opportunity for enjoyment, challenge, self-expression, and social interaction.

Introduction

Whether it is ice, field, floor, roller, or broom, hockey is a popular team sport that can be played by both males and females. It is sport that offers many challenges to middle school students. These challenges include a wide range of ball handling skills, offensive and defensive game strategies, and fitness opportunities.

In a hockey unit, the following fundamentals can be covered: forehand and reverse stick grips, dribbling, fielding, passing and shooting (drive, push, scoop), tackling and dodging, basic offensive and defensive game strategies, goal keeping, rules, and safety.

Warm-up Ideas

1. ***All Lines***. Each student has a ball and a stick. Students dribble around the entire hockey field keeping their ball close to the lines that mark the playing field. If they must pass another student on the same line, they must use a dodge to the stick or non-stick side.

2. ***Hockey Hunt***. Students should find a partner who has the same skill level. Both students should have a ball and a stick. One partner begins in the center of the field and is designated as "it". The other partner can begin anywhere within the boundaries of the playing field. On the "go" signal, both partners begin to dribble. The object is for the "it" to find and successfully tag his/her partner. Once the partner has been tagged, that person stands and does 10 cross-over dribbles in 10 place. The other person dribbles away from the partner while he/she is doing cross-over dribble. Once 10 dribbles have been completed, that person chases his/her partner. Continue for two minutes.

Station Ideas

1. *Hockey Hub*. Divide the students into groups of four. Before class, the teacher should write down various hockey skills on index cards. These cards are placed in a box in the center of the field. This center known as the "The Hub." Group members take turns running to The Hub to retrieve a card. When the person returns to the group with the card, the group members perform the skill(s) indicated on the card. After the group finishes the task, a new group member runs the card back to the box and selects a new task card. Continue for five minutes. Examples of skill activities are listed below. Music can be made to indicate transitions for students. Thirty to 60 seconds of music can provide students with an opportunity to perform as many repetitions as possible. Ten to 15 seconds of silence can be used to retrieve a new card.

TASK CARDS

- Place your hockey stick on the ground. Jump back and forth over your stick 30 times.
- With a partner, move across the field performing push passes.
- Air dribble using one or all sides of you hockey stick (try for 10 dribbles without a miss).
- Do 25 sit-ups with a partner while passing a hockey stick back and forth.
- Invent three safe stretches using your hockey stick.
- In a square, see how many consecutive push passes can be made in 30 seconds.
- Zigzag dribble in and out of the cones.
- Using reverse stick, do 20 push passes to your partner.
- Keeping the ball below your knees, lift the ball to your partner 15 times.
- Practice dodging partner on his/her stick and non-stick side.

Lead-up Games and Fitness Activities

1. **_Star Drill_**. Five students form a star and are given a number (one to five). Number one passes to number two, two to three, three to four, four to five, and five to one. After passing the ball, the passer follows the pass and takes that person's spot. The object of the activity is to see how quickly the group can return to their original place. The activity can be played against other groups or against the clock.

2. **_Hockey Race Track_**. Students work in pairs. One partner performs a hockey skill in a designated area while the other partner jogs around the perimeter of all the other students. This perimeter is called the "Hockey Race Track." When the jogger returns home, the partners switch places. Signs can be posted to indicate the next skill to be performed.

3. **_Three-Person Weave_**. Students get in groups of three and form a single-file line. The ball is started by the center person and passed to either the person on the left or the right. The person passing the ball will always run behind the person receiving the pass (pass and follow). The person receiving the pass takes the ball to the center position and then passes to the other person. This procedure continues until they reach the other end line. Students can end with a shot at the goal.

4. **_Triangle Away_**. Divide the class into groups of four. Each group should form a triangle with one person in the middle. Use cones to mark the triangle. This will help students stay spread out. The students forming the triangle try to keep the ball away from the center person. Students may only push pass to each other. After one minute, rotate the middle person.

5. **_Tackle Box._** Students work in groups of four. Cones should be used to designate a 10-yard by 5-yard box. This area is the "Tackle Box." Select one student from each group to be the defender inside the Tackle Box. The other three students are offensive players and try, one at a time, to get their ball through the Tackle Box. Rotate the defensive player every minute.

6. **_Catch Up_**. Three students are designated as offensive players, and two students are defensive players. The three offensive players line up 5 yards in front of the defensive players. Everyone races to the goal cage (50 yards away). The offensive players start with a ball and try to get the ball in the goal. The defensive players attempt to catch up and take the ball away from them.

7. **_No Goalie Hockey_**. This game is played like regular hockey, except there is no goalie. The length of the field should be shortened (play the width of the field) and use cones for the goal.

8. **_End Zone Hockey_**. The entire end line of the field is the goal area. Each team designates a certain number of goalies and field players. The goalies must spread out over the entire goal line area in order to protect it. Goalies and field players should change places every two minutes.

Conclusion

Hockey is an excellent team game for middle school students. It is an activity that can improve the students' cardiovascular endurance while engaging them in activity that develops cooperation and teamwork. Students will find that hockey is both a challenging and enjoyable activity.

References

Pangrazi, R. P., and Darst, P.W. (In Press). _Dynamic Physical Education for Secondary School Students_. 3 rd edition. Boston, MA: Allyn and Bacon Publishing Co.
The Eagle. Official publication of the United State Field Hockey Association, Inc. Mark G. Whitney, Editor.

Soccer: It's on the Move!

By Margie L. Miller
Skaith Elementary School
St. Joseph, MO

National Standards

✐ Demonstrates competency in many movement forms and proficiency in a few movement forms.
✐ Exhibits a physically active lifestyle.
✐ Achieves and maintains a health-enhancing level of physical fitness.

Introduction

Soccer is an excellent activity to develop cardiovascular endurance. In order to achieve this objective the teacher, must maximize participation by modifying traditional soccer to include exciting lead-up games and plenty of equipment. Activities that will motivate students to improve the basic skills of soccer and, at the same time, improve cardiovascular fitness are listed below.

Warm-up and Flexibility Activities

The warm-up and conditioning activities listed below can be done with a soccer ball or any type of utility or soccer-size nerf ball.

1. Juggling is an activity that satisfies the student's natural desire to immediately pick up a ball and do something with it. In addition, juggling activities can be easily modified to present challenges to a wide range of skill level. Each student should have a ball and enough personal space so that he/she does not interfere with other students. Challenge students to juggle or bounce the ball on a specified body part and then catch it. The knees are the easiest body part with which to begin. When a student can accomplish one juggle and a catch, add two juggles, then three juggles, etc. After the students have practiced with the knee, have them try, juggling with the foot or head.

2. Each student should have a ball. Have the students place the balls on ground. On a signal from the teacher, they should begin to jump back and forth over the ball with both feet. Time the students for 30 seconds and have them count the number of times they are able to jump over the ball.. Repeat the activity and challenge the students to get at least one more jump than they got the first time.

3. Each student stands in a stride position with the ball held overhead. Stretch to the right side and touch the right foot and then the left foot. Stretch up to the left side of the body and then stretch to the right side of the body. After stretching to the right twice, reverse directions and stretch to the left side of the body.

4. Several stretches can be done with the students sifting on the ground.
   - Students sit with their legs outstretched in front of them. Students should roll the ball around the legs and then around the back.
   - Students have legs outstretched in front of the body and place the ball at their feet. Stretch slowly toward the ball and hold for at least 10 seconds.

   - Students sit in a modified straddle position (one leg extended and the other leg bent). Place the ball at the foot of the extended leg and stretch toward the ball. Switch leg positions and repeat the stretch.
   - Students lie on their backs with their arms and legs outstretched. Place the ball between the feet and lift the ball up with the feet. Students reach up to their feet and remove the ball and touch the ball to the ground behind their head with their hands. They should then take the ball and put it back between the feet and return hands and feet to the ground.

Lead-up Activities and Fitness Development

1. _**Marking**_. Students are in pairs with a ball for every pair. One partner will run and dribble the ball through an area while the other follows. The dribbler tries to lose the partner without the ball. On a signal, players freeze and, at this point, the followers must be able to touch the dribblers. Switch places and repeat the sequence. After several trials, ask the students to describe what it means to mark an opponent.

2. _**Tackling**_. Students are in pairs with a ball for every pair. One partner will run and dribble the soccer ball while the other partner attempts to steal the ball by using proper tackling techniques. If the ball is stolen, the person who stole the ball dribbles and the other partner tries to tackle.

3. _**Dribbling Activities**_. Divide the class in half. Half of the students have a ball and the other half form a tunnel by standing in a stride position anywhere in a specified area. The students with the balls dribble to the players who are forming a tunnel and pass the ball between their legs. When a ball passes through a tunnel, the person forming the tunnel must drop into a crab position. When another ball passes under a person in a crab positions, he/she once again becomes a tunnel. Players with the ball count the number of tunnels and crabs they pass the ball through. Time the activity for one minute. Have the students repeat this activity in the same positions and challenge the dribblers to get to five more tunnels than they did the first time. Switch places and have the tunnels be the dribblers and the dribblers, be the tunnels. A variation of this activity is to see how long it takes each half of the class to dribble through all the

tunnels. A tunnel is closed when five balls have been passed through it. When a tunnel closes, the tunnel player holds the up position of a push-up. Try to see which half of the class can close the tunnels the quickest.

4. ***Guard the Pin***. Divide the class in half. Half of the students are dribblers and shooters, and the other half are guards. Use bowling pins, Pringles cans, tennis cans, or milk cartons for targets. All guards should have a pin and should find a spot to place the pin in a specified area. The guards stand next to and protect their pin. They may only use their feet, torso, or head (no hands) to protect the pin. On a signal, the dribblers attempt to knock as many pins over as possible in a given time. When a pin is knocked over, the guard immediately sets it back up. At the end of the time period, add up all pins that have been knocked over and switch places.

Conclusion

Soccer is an activity that most students find motivating and challenging. It is also a great activity to develop cardiovascular endurance without the students ever knowing it. By increasing the number of balls and simplifying the rules, students can get an extensive workout in a short period of time while still developing skill.

Soccer

By John L. Smith
Ho-Ho-Kus Elementary School
Ho-Ho-Kus, NJ

National Standards

🖋 Demonstrates competency in many movement forms and proficiency in a few movement forms.
🖋 Applies movement concepts and principles to the learning and development of motor skills.

Introduction

The soccer ladder is a way of using the skills that the students have been practicing in a game-like, teacher controlled situation. This activity provides the teacher with flexibility to view the students' skill development. The ladder improves students' motivation, develops equal and fair competition, and allows for ample practice of skills.

Soccer Ladder

The ladder is set up by placing cones or markers 10 yards apart to form one playing field for one game. These cones or markers serve as the goals for that field. As many playing fields as necessary to service a full class can be set up 10 yards apart. The field diagram for four playing fields follows:

Field One	Field Two	Field Three	Field Four
Cone	Cone	Cone	Cone
10 yards	10 yards	10 yards	10 yards
Cone	Cone	Cone	Cone

(Each playing field is 10 yards away from the next playing field.)

Soccer Ladder
Dribble and pass your way up the soccer ladder of success

The game may be played as a one-on-one game. A player defends his/her own cone while trying to attack and score at the opponent's goal. A goal is scored when the ball touches the opponent's cone. The games are limited to two minutes each. At the end of two minutes, successful players move up the ladder while the unsuccessful players move down the ladder. If the score is tied at the end of the time limit, the player in control of the ball is declared the successful player and moves up the ladder. Neither player will remain at the same playing field for two games in a row. After four or five games, players should be playing against opponents of equal ability.

The teacher may change any rules at any time to improve the learning experience. Ways in which the teacher can change the game include lengthening the game, increasing the numbers of cones a player must defend, or increasing the size of the playing field. The game may also be played as a two-on-two team competition.

Conclusion

The skill of dribbling is used most during the one-on-one games. In the two-on-two games, the skills of passing, receiving, and counter-attacking come into play. No matter which game is played, the students receive beneficial soccer skills practice and a cardiovascular workout.

Fitness Kickball

By Meggin DeMoss
Seltzer Elementary School
Wichita, KS

National Standards

- Exhibits a physically active lifestyle.
- Achieves and maintains a health-enhancing level of physical fitness.
- Understands that physical activity provides the opportunity for enjoyment, challenge, self-expression, and social interaction.

Introduction

Kickball has long been placed in the "Hall of Shame" as an activity that is not appropriate at the middle school level. The game, in its original form, lacks any developmental appropriateness past the fourth grade. Fitness kickball, however, adds dimensions that allow for the development of teamwork and strategies, as well as contributing to the fitness levels of the students involved.

Activity Description

Divide the class into two teams. One team is at bat and the other is the fielding team. The teacher pitches. A box with six playground or other kicking balls is placed next to the teacher. The teacher rolls a ball to the first batter, who kicks the ball and begins to run the bases. As soon as the first batter begins to run, the teacher takes another ball from the box and pitches it. As the second batter kicks and begins to run the bases, the teacher again takes a ball from the box and pitches it for the third batter. The batting team is trying to kick and run the bases as fast as possible. There may be more than one base runner running at a time. Base runners may not pass each other and may not stop on a base.

75

As the balls are being kicked into the field, the fielders are trying to retrieve the balls and place them back in the box as quickly as possible. The fielding team must never allow the box to become empty. If the box becomes empty, the batting team receives three points.

Each batter will receive only one pitch to kick. If a batter misses the ball, that player must retrieve the ball and bring it to the box. The fielding team is never penalized for an empty box if a batting team has a ball.

During each inning every player kicks the ball one time. As the last kicker comes to bat, he/she must call out "last batter." The last batter kicks and begins to run the bases. This last batter tries to run all four bases before the fielding team can get all six balls back into the box. When all six balls are back in the box, the fielding team yells "stop." At this point, the score is recorded for the batting team.

A team may score points by doing any of the following:

1. A batter crossing homeplate after running the bases receives one point.
2. The last batter gets five points for crossing homeplate before all six balls are in the box.
3. The batting team gets three points every time there is not at least one ball in the box.

The teams have 15 seconds to change places before the first ball is pitched. This rule reinforces the quick change from offense to defense. After playing a couple of innings, reduce the number of balls in the box by one, but never go lower than three balls in the box.

Conclusion

Fitness kickball is an active game in which all students must participate. Unlike the standard game of kickball, every player must kick each inning, run the bases, and field kicked balls. Teamwork and cooperation tendered with a spirit of competition makes this game a middle school favorite.

 # S◯FTBALL

By Kathy Ermler
Emporia State University
Emporia, KS

National Standards

✎ Demonstrates competency in many movement forms and proficiency in a few movement forms.
✎ Understands that physical activity provides the opportunity for enjoyment, challenge, self-expression, and social interaction.

Introduction

Softball is an activity found in many middle school programs. However, in many cases most of the activity is performed by only a few players, while many others just stand and watch. The following softball variations allow for every student to become an active participant.

Snake Softball

This game teaches students the order of the positions in softball as they practice throwing in the correct order to each defensive position. The game begins by a batter hitting or throwing the ball into the field. This batter runs to first base. As soon as this player rounds first, the next runner on the batting team begins running. This process continues through the entire lineup.

While the batting team is running the bases, the fielding team is retrieving the hit. The ball must be returned to the pitcher, who then begins the throwing sequence from one position to the next in order. (Example: Position 1=pitcher, 2=catcher, 3=first base, etc.) When the fielding team completes the throwing rotation, they yell "stop!" The fielding team quickly shifts one position, and the batting teams hits again. The batting team gets to hit three times. The batting team's score is the number of people who have crossed homeplate in the three outs. The teams have 15 seconds to exchange places and the game continues.

Five Player Softball

This variation is an excellent warm-up activity for softball. The object is to see how many times each person can bat in a three-minute time period. Each team consists of five players. Assign each player one of following positions: catcher, pitcher, batter, fielder 1#, or fielder #2. The batter gets one pitch to hit. As soon as the pitch is hit, everyone on the team rotates as quickly as possible to the next position (see diagram below) while trying to retrieve the ball and returning it to the next pitcher. Equipment needed for each team is a pillo pollo bat or whiffle bat and a 12-inch diameter nerf ball. Play for two to three minutes. Bunts can also be practiced in this formation.

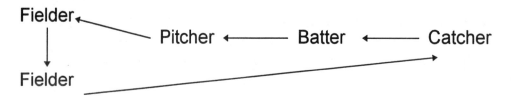

Basketbase

This variation is played with a basketball which is thrown into the field by the batting team. The batting team begins to run the bases in the same fashion as in snake softball. While the batting team is running, the fielding team gets the ball and everyone must perform a lay-up (free-throw, set shot, etc.). When everyone has shot the ball, the fielding team yells "stop!" Both the offensive as well as the defensive team can score. The fielding team gets one point for each lay-up they make, and the batting team gets one point for each person who crosses home plate. The batting team gets three throws before it becomes the defense.

Conclusion

These softball variations allow all students to develop skills in fielding and throwing. The variations also allow for some fitness enhancement through skill development.

3 on 3 Basketball Games: Skills and Thrills

By John L. Smith
Ho-Ho-Kus Elementary School
Ho-Ho-Kus, NJ

National Standards

- Demonstrates competency in many movement forms and proficiency in a few movement forms.
- Applies movement concepts and principles to the learning and development of motor skills.
- Demonstrates understanding and respect for differences among people in physical activity settings.

Introduction

This activity idea can be used at any time during a basketball unit, but it is an excellent end-of-the-unit activity. The activity allows for a culmination of all the skills learned or for the development of a single skill. It can also provide an arena for skill testing through a rubric type evaluation.

Class Organization

After the students have completed their warm-up, the games begin. The class should be divided into teams of three people. This may be accomplished in several ways. The teacher may organize the teams before coming to class, use skill evaluations, or divide the students by position. Try to select a method that will get students into the activity quickly.

Game Situations

Each game will last between two and three minutes. At the end of the allotted time, teams rotate to different baskets to play different teams. This rotation can be accomplished by keeping one team at each basket and rotating the other team. If the game is tied after the time limit, identify one person from each team to shoot a lay-up or foul shot. The first team to make the shot is the winner.

The uniqueness of this activity lies in the flexibility given to the teacher to create a learning environment with rule changes. The teacher can change the amount or time, the type of shot allowed, the number of dribbles that can be used, the passes that must be completed before the shot, or who can shoot the ball. With rule changes like these the teacher can take the team's leading scorer and make him/her a passer and rebounder. The student that never shoots now feels that he/she is needed by the team.

Another great rule change is to have the opponents choose the players on the opposite team who cannot score except on an offensive rebound or whose points are worth double value. Again, this takes the "best" individual player and makes him/her a team player, as well as giving the novice player value to the team and an opportunity to develop needed skills.

The best time to make rule changes is after three or four rotations. This gives the teams a chance to play and learn about their team before they make change.

Conclusion

This activity takes little effort to incorporate into a basketball unit. However, it offers tremendous potential for the development of learned skills, strategic planning, and teamwork. This idea can also be adapted to other team games.

TEAM PICKLE-BALL

By Rickey Parris
Mann Middle School
Abilene, TX

National Standards

✏ Demonstrates competency in many movement forms and proficiency in a few movement forms.
✏ Understands that physical activity provides the opportunity for enjoyment, challenge, self-expression, and social interaction.

Introduction

Pickle-Ball is a game originally developed as a family activity in 1965 by William Bell, Barney McCallum, and U.S. Congressman Joel Pritchard. It is a supremely popular racquet sport with middle school physical education students. This popularity may be due to either the relative ease that students have in mastering the skill, or to the satisfying noise made by the contact of a wooden paddle on a plastic ball. With simple adaptations to the traditional singles and doubles racket sport games, a "team" game can be developed that provides maximum participation in large physical education classes.

Station Activities

Stations provide an excellent way to review skills and give students a chance to practice their skills in a nonthreatening manner. Try to keep the number of students per station small. Have students work on the stations listed below for 30 seconds and then move to the next station.

Station 1:   Ball Handling. In this drill, the student should perform controlled upward bounces off the paddle to strengthen the forehand grip. As skill level improves, students should try flip-flopping the paddle to alternate the hitting surface during the upward bounces. Poly spots or hula hoops can be used as home Positions. These spots encourage the students to keep control of the ball.

Station 2: Drop, Hit, Catch. Students should stand about 10-20 feet from the wall. Students should drop and then hit the ball to the wall and then catch the ball after it bounces one time. Students will need to be shown the way to catch the ball. They should catch it with one hand and close the paddle over the ball hand. In addition to developing drive shots, this drill is important in teaching the rule that prohibits volleying before the serve and service return have bounced.

Station 3: Serves. Students should straddle a serving line located 15-20 feet from the wall and attempt to serve into a target (hula hoop) three to five feet high. The server follows the same procedure as in the previous drill, but the ball is hit underhand, without a bounce. Students attempt to see how many serves they can make in 30 seconds.

Station 4: Wall Rally with Volleys. Establish a restraining line 5-10 feet from the wall. Students stand behind this line and attempt to volley the ball back to the wall. Make sure the students understand that if they step over the line to volley, they have entered the no-volley zone and have committed an infraction in Pickle-Ball.

Lead-up Activities

In addition to the previous individual and partner drills, the following lead-up activities can be used to practice skills of Pickle-Ball in a game-like environment.

Alley Rally. This is an excellent activity to improve the students' concentration and accuracy. Students should find a partner and stand on a line three feet apart. Each student should have a racquet and a ball. The students place the ball in front of their feet to serve as a target. A third ball is put into play with a soft hit. The object of the game is to try to hit the third ball so that it lands on the other player's ball-target. Students are not allowed to guard their target. Smashing is also not allowed. The  players alternate attempts after each bounce with a soft upward stroke. They should attempt to keep rallying back and forth and not catch the ball unless they have lost control of it.

Backhand Bumps. This game is designed to develop the correct follow-through on backhands. Students should find a partner and designate one person as the hitter and the other as the tosser. The hitter, using a backhand grip, stands on a line 10 feet from the tosser. The paddle is placed at the knees. The tosser bounces a ball in front of the hitter. The hitter's objective is to return the ball with a backhand follow-through motion by raising the hitting arm to shoulder level.. The return is successful if the tosser can catch the ball before it bounces and without moving his/her feet. After five attempts, the players switch roles.

Smash. This drill develops the offensive skills of smashing and putting the ball out of play. Students should find a partner and designate one person as the hitter and the other as the tosser. The hitter stands at the no-volley line with a paddle in the "backscratch" position associated with hitting overhead shots. A tosser, positioned to the side and slightly in front of the hitter, softly tosses balls to the forehand side (8-12 feet high) so that the hitter can attempt to smash into the opponent's court. Students should observe the restraints of the non-volley zones. Feet are not to cross the restraining line during the drill. The difficulty of this drill can be increased by having targets located on the floor. The students should attempt to direct the smash into these targets.

Conclusion

By combining the game of Pickle-Ball with age-appropriate stations and lead-up activities, the middle school physical educator can successfully keep large classes on-task as students master the skills of this unique racquet sport.

IDEAS III:

Section Four

Rhythms and Gymnastics

Rhythm Ideas For the Less Than Ideal Dancer

By Joella Mehrhof
Emporia State University
Emporia, KS

National Standards

- Demonstrates responsible personal and social behavior in physical activity settings.
- Understands that physical activity provides the opportunity for enjoyment, challenge, self-
- expression, and social interaction.

Introduction

Dance and rhythmic activity are a very important part of the middle school physical education curriculum. However, this area is often neglected for a variety of reasons. These reasons may include things such as the self-consciousness of the students, the lack of experience in dance of the students, the teacher's lack of knowledge of appropriate dance content, and the music to use in this unit. By using nonthreatening activities with simple movements patterns, dance and rhythms can be incorporated into the middle school curriculum. The following are two ideas to introduce dance at this level.

Rhythmic Tennis Ball Passing

The old saying "there is power in numbers" may apply to the teaching of dance and rhythms. By introducing a rhythmic activity where a group of people are a team and by putting a familiar piece of equipment in each student's hand, the teacher may find the "power" to motivate the middle school student.

Rhythmic tennis ball passing is performed by a group of six to eight students standing in a circle. Each student has a tennis ball in his/her right hand. Simple passing patterns are introduced and performed to music with a peppy 4/4 beat. Sample passing patterns include:

Pattern 1:	Pass the ball to the right every two counts.
Pattern 2:	Pass the ball to the right on counts 1 and 2, and then lift it in the air on counts 3 and 4.
Pattern 3:	Lift the ball on counts 1 and 2, pass the ball around the waist on counts 3 and 4, lift it in the air on counts 5 and 6, and pass to the right on counts 7 and 8.
Pattern 4:	Four passes between own hands for 4 counts and then pass to the right twice on the next 4 counts.
Pattern 5:	Take the ball around the neck on counts 1 and 2, set it on the head on counts 3 and 4, turn around in place on counts 5 and 6, and pass it to the right on counts 7 and 8.

Teach one pattern at a time. After one pattern is mastered, teach the next pattern. After the second pattern is mastered, combine pattern one and pattern two by performing each pattern four times. Continue to add new patterns and combine patterns after they have been introduced.

Other patterns may be created by the students. Encourage them to create an eight-count pattern that can be repeated. Give them hints for organizing new movement phrases. The following movement hints may spark the creative juices:

- Try moving around the circle while passing the tennis ball.
- Try moving into the center of the circle and back while passing the ball.
- Try taking the ball around various body parts before passing it.
- Try putting a bounce in the pattern.
- Try reversing a pattern.
- Try putting a jump into the pattern.

Partner Line Dancing

Line dancing has become a popular activity because many of the dances have easy and similar steps. However, there is very little social interaction in a line dance, since most of the dances do not require partners. With a partner line dance, the dance remains simple, but students dance with another person in a nonthreatening manner. The following are the steps to a simple partner line dance. The dance is performed in two lines facing.

➢ Grapevine to the right and then left (8 counts)
➢ Three-step turn to the right and three-step turn to the left (8 counts)
➢ Step right and touch left, step left and touch right (4 counts)
➢ Step right and touch left, step left and touch right (4 counts)
➢ Right heel touches front twice, kick right foot to the front and step right (4 counts)
➢ Left heel touches front twice, kick left foot to the front and step left (4 counts)
➢ Walk forward 3 counts and the give the partner a high five on count 4
➢ Walk backward 4 counts
➢ Walk forward and "boogie around" your partner and back to place (do-si-do) in 8 counts
➢ Walk forward 4 counts and do a "low ten" four times (slapping both hands and turning them over each time) with the partner
➢ Walk backward 4 counts and do a pivot turn for 4 counts

Suggested music for the partner line dance includes "Bounce to the Beat" by CC Music Factory; "Sight for Sore Eyes" by M People; "Ain't Never Gonna Give You Up" by Paula Abdul; or "We Are Family" by Sister Sledge.

Conclusion

Dance and rhythmic activity can be fun and a tremendous opportunity for social skill development. The use of music that is familiar to the middle school student increases the opportunity for success. Dance and rhythms should be approached with a smile and a sense of humor.

Tinikling and Jump Bands

By Nannette Wolford
Missouri Western State College
St. Joseph, MO

National Standards

- Exhibits a physically active lifestyle.
- Achieves and maintains a health-enhancing level of physical fitness.
- Understands that physical activity provides the opportunity for enjoyment, challenge, self-expression, and social interaction.

Introduction

Activities using Tinikling poles and jump bands help to develop rhythm, cardiovascular endurance, muscular strength, and coordination. These activities can be used with any size group and allow group members of different skill levels to progress at their own speed.

Teachers may want to share a brief history of Tinikling with their students. Tinikling is a folk dance from the Philippines. The dancer is mimicking the rice bird running from one rice paddy to another. While the original dance was done to music with 3/4 time, the activities suggested in this article use music with 4/4 time. The polers originally used bamboo poles for the dance. However, PVC pipe, cut in 8-foot lengths, is more durable and cheaper to use. Two wooden 1 x 1 cross bars cut in 12 inch lengths, should be used to help protect the polers hands.

Jump bands are an invention that imitates the Tinikling poles. The jump bands are made of elastic-like material with a loop at each end. The loops are for the polers' feet. The polers place their feet in the loops and jump the rhythm pattern of two counts straddle and two counts with feet together. These jump bands allow for the fitness development of both the jumpers and polers.

Tinikling Warm-up Activities

Set the poles in a line (similar to a football tire agility drill) so the students can run through them. Possible activities the students can do with this set-up include:

- Run through the poles stepping in and out down the poles.
- Jump in and out the poles.
- Hop in and out with the same leg down the line and come back hopping on the other leg.
- Leap over each set of poles reaching and stretching with arms and legs.

Jump Band Warm-up Activities

Place the jump bands on cones in a maze fashion. Designate two or three people to be "it" and give each of "its" a bean bag. The "its" must tag someone with their bean bag. The players must follow the jump band, but may go any direction and jump over the bands to the other side. The players may also jump from line to line to escape the persons who are it. After the person who is "it" tags someone, he/she places the bean bag on the floor and the person who was tagged picks up the bean bag and becomes the new "it." No student is ever eliminated from this activity. If a student steps on or hits a jump band while trying to escape, he/she automatically becomes "it."

Tinikling Steps

Polers. Polers should practice performing and maintaining the correct beat. The polers should take the poles and tap them together for two beats and then slide them apart and tap the cross bar for two beats (cues could be "down, down, up, up" or "together, apart"). Remind the polers not to lift the poles too much and to tap them together lightly. When polers separate the poles, instruct them to take the poles to the very end of the cross bar.

Basic Dance Steps

Basic Step. The dancer begins on the outside of the poles with the right foot closest to the poles. On the first two counts or while the poles are together, the dancer hops twice on the left foot. On count three, the dancer steps into the center of the poles with the right foot. On count four, the dancer steps into the center of the poles with the left foot. Repeat all of the above on the other side.

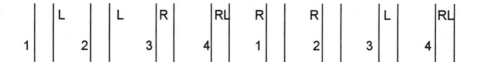

Doubles.   The dancer begins on the outside of the poles with the right foot closest to the poles. On the two counts, the dancer jumps on both feet outside the poles. On the next two counts, the dancer jumps on both feet inside the poles. Repeat to the other sides

	RL	RL	RL		RL
Counts	Counts	Counts	Counts
1,2	3,4	1,2	3,4

Hop Step.   While standing on the outside of the poles, hop twice on the left foot. On the next two counts, hop twice on the right foot. Repeat.

	L Hop	R		L	R
Counts	Counts	Counts	Counts
1, 2	3,4	1, 2	3,4

92

Advanced Dance Steps. The following steps add variation to the basic dance step.

High 5: With a partner, clap partner's hands above the head outside the bands (counts 1 and 2) and slap the thighs inside the bands (counts 3 and 4).

Face Off. When using the jump bands, the jumper faces the poler. When the jumper is outside the bands (counts 1 and 2), slap thighs, when inside the bands (counts 3 and 4), clap polers hands.

Centipede. With a line of four students, start with one dance and add a dancer each time they return until all are dancing. Have them place their hands on the person's shoulders in front of them.

Inside Outside. This move is similar to the straddle step except the dancer steps one foot at a time between the bands.

| 1 | R | 2 | L | 3 | R | L 4 | 1 | R | 2 | L | 3 | R | L 4 |

Home Base. This is a cross formation and is performed with four dancers. Use the basic step and begin with the right foot closest to the bands.

Visiting the Neighbors. The jumpers travel around the home base pattern stepping right, left, right, left, until they are back to their home base (original spot).

Jaws. Dancers all start in a line in one area and travel through the center. They then rotate to the right until all four areas have been used and the center crossed through.

Box Cars. Polers form three sets of bands/poles. The dancers can move down the box cars any fashion they desire.

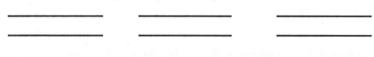

Variations. Once these basic steps are mastered, various formations can be made. Let your students be creative. Here are a few examples.

Cross or T
(Go around or through the middle)

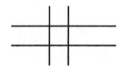

Rectangle

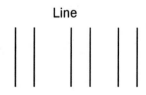

Triangle

Line

Conclusion

Tinikling and jump bands provide fun with a rhythmic challenge. After learning the basics, students can create new patterns using such equipment as balls, jump ropes, and hoops. These activities are also great for cardiovascular endurance improvement.

References

Pangrazi, Robert, P., and Dauer, Victor, P., (1995). *Dynamic Physical Education for Elementary School Children*. Allyn and Bacon Inc. Needham Heights, MA.
Pexton, D. Boyd, (1995). *Contemporary Tinikling Activities*. Kimbo Educational , Long Branch, N. J.
Short, Kathryn, (1993). *Jump Bands*. Physical Education Activity Video, Katheryn Short Productions, Phone.

Educational Gymnastics: An Opportunity for Interdependence and Individual Ingenuity

By Fran Cleland
West Chester State University
West Chester, PA

National Standards

✎ Demonstrates competency in many movement forms and proficiency in a few movement forms.
✎ Applies movement concepts and principles to the learning and development of motor skills.
✎ Understands that physical activity provides the opportunity for enjoyment, challenge, self-expression, and social interaction.

Introduction

All aspects of an educational gymnastics lesson should relate to the lesson's theme. The warm-up, stations, equipment selection, and sequence of movement tasks should follow a logical progression. Objectives of the lesson, which reflect the theme, may focus on 1) fitness development, 2) conceptual understanding of the theme, 3) ability to connect individual movements, or 4) observation skills.

The following are some sample lessons based on different themes. The material of each sample lesson includes, 1) warm-up, 2) station ideas, 3) equipment selection, 4) lead-up activities and related fitness skills. These lessons are designed to accommodate large classes. Organization of students into small groups often facilitates experimentation in response to gymnastic problems.

LESSON THEME 1   Skill: Jumping and Landing
Movement Concepts: Bend, Stretch, and Twist

Warm-up Ideas

➡ Students bend, stretch, and twist their bodies in their own personal space.

➡ Holding ropes taut in hands within their own space, students perform bent, stretched, and twisted shapes.

➡ Place jump ropes on the floor. These ropes can be flush with floor or suspended from small cones. Students can begin the lesson by bending, stretching, and/or twisting as they balance on both hands and feet, one hand and two feet, or two hands and one foot. Emphasis would be placed on making big and wide shapes.

➡ Same as above, but change equipment to folded mats. Students perform bent, stretch, and/or twisted positions over mats or with body partially on/off mat.

➡ Same as above using hula-hoops positioned obstacles on three cones, vertically positioned using hoop-holder, or flush with the floor.

Lead-up Activities

➡ Students perform jumps with light force across ropes flush to floor, or horizontally suspended from low objects such as cones. While performing the jump, students should combine the movement concepts of bending, stretching, and twisting movements.

➡ Several low obstacles are placed throughout the gym. These might include stools, jumping boxes, folded mats, ropes suspended horizontally, low benches, or hula-hoops. Students perform the same activity as above in relationship to these obstacles. Several individual jumps (e.g., three different jumps) can then be combined to form a phrase.

➠ Students perform jumps with light force off low objects. Emphasis is placed on execution of bent, stretched, or twisted positions or shapes in air, prior to landing.

➠ Students then select three different pieces of equipment (e.g., hula-hoop, cones, ropes, and folded mat). Partner groups could design a "movement track" with their equipment. This track could follow a straight or curved line. Partners could then develop a jumping sentence combining each of their ideas. These sequences could be performed in 1) "unison", 2) "meeting and parting", or 3) "passing each other." The sequence could also include a "point of stillness" to add variation. This could also be conducted with groups of three and four students.

➠ Jumping sequences using equipment could then combine some relationship elements such as jumping off, over, across, or through in conjunction with bent, stretched, and twisted shapes.

Station Ideas

Station 1
Equipment: Rolled up wrestling mat with floor mats placed for landing.

Suggested movement problem: Using *medium to strong force* find as many different ways to jump off the mat as possible. Landings should be soft, with weight evenly distributed on feet, knees bent to absorb force, and body weight under control.

Station 2
Equipment: Three jump ropes suspended horizontally on low cones, about three feet apart

Suggested movement problem: Design a phrase using three different jumps performed quickly over the ropes. The jumps should flow together, one right after the other. Be sure to have a clear beginning and ending position (these could be balances students have previously created and practiced).

Station 3

Equipment: Tires arranged in a pattern. Students could create this, pattern before they perform at this station.

Suggested movement problem: Can you discover different jumps in and out or over the tires? Can these jumps change direction?

Station 4

Equipment: German vaulting box or bench.

Suggested movement problem: Find ways of jumping and landing off the vault or bench using the movement concepts of bend, stretch or twist. Connect jumps by performing a slow stretching or twisting action with the body to get back onto the bench or vault.

Station 5

Equipment: Hula-hoop and hoop-holder, jump rope, folded mat, three tires. Students arrange equipment into a "track".

Suggested movement problem: Create a combination of jumps as you travel along or through your movement track. You can perform individually or with partners where partners meet and part or pass each other.

Station 6

Equipment: Floor mat.

Suggested movement problem: Perform five different jumps on the mat with at least one locomotor pattern between each jump.

Warm-up Ideas

Equipment for Warm-ups

➟ The warm-up activities require floor mats and pieces of equipment to perform counter-tension balances. Hanging ropes, bars attached to the wall, or benches could be used.

➟ Individual students perform different counter-tension balances (leaning away from) by gripping onto hanging ropes, weighted benches, balance beam, or bars. The equipment serves as each student's partner. Balances with upper and lower body parts could be discovered.

➟ Using only the upper body (i.e., elbows, wrists, hands), partners try to perform different counter tension balances, controlling each other's weight by finding a point of equilibrium (e.g., elbow to elbow, partners leaning away; hand to wrist, one partner high, one partner low while leaning away; back to back using hands to wrists and leaning outward). The same tasks could also be used to create different counterbalances where partners control each other's weight while leaning toward each other (e.g., hands to hands, back to back, side to side, etc.).

Lead-up Activities

➟ Continuing with the theme of counterbalances, students could perform balances on three or more body parts. Partners could discover additional types of counterbalances, varying the balances using different levels.

➟ Students can perform rolls, locomotor skills, or transfer weight from hands to feet (i.e., previously learned skills) into and out of any of the balances designed in the above warm-ups.

- Students can create several counterbalances and then determine how to move from one counterbalance to another under control. Again, locomotor patterns into and out of the beginning and ending counterbalance could add to making a completed movement sentence.

- The movement concept of symmetrical and asymmetrical could be an added element to the above lead-ups.

Additional partnering activities
1. Helping a partner to jump.
2. Matching another person's movements.
3. Supporting another partner with varying bases of support.
4. Using a partner as an obstacle: under, over, around.

LESSON THEME 3	**Skill: Locomotor - Transfer of Weight**
Movement Concepts:	**Pathways, Level, Direction, Speed, Relationships**

Warm-up Ideas

- Using previously learned skills involving rolling on floor mats, students perform rolling actions up to different balanced positions. Balances could be at high, medium, or low levels and be on any number of body parts.

- Add the speed changes to the above. Students begin slowly and then add speed as they roll into balanced positions.

- Students could also revisit support of weight on hands and feet. This movement task must be phrased to include all ability levels. Therefore, asking students to execute handstands would be inappropriate. However, asking students to find ways to support their weight using hands and/or feet at different levels would be appropriate. In addition the teacher could add rocking or tilting into and out of balanced positions.

Station Ideas

Station 1

Using tires placed far apart on the floor or on mats, students perform transferring weight from hands to feet on and off of the tires.

Station 2

With jump ropes on floor or suspended at low levels, students discover at least three different ways to travel over each rope. This may include transfer of weight from hands to feet, and/or include different types of locomotor possibilities using feet only.

Station 3

Using a folded mat or vaulting box, students perform different types of weight transfer over the obstacle. Hands can be used to propel body over mat or box, landing on feet. Walking and running starts can also be incorporated. Students should be encouraged to use the sides and top of mats or the box.

Station 4

Using floor mats only, students concentrate on combining two or three types of weight transfer as they travel down the length or back and forth across width of the mat. For example, students could be prompted to create a phrase combining three different types of weight transfer including, a) from hands to feet, b) a rolling action, and c) a locomotor pattern on one or two feet.

Station 5

Using a partner or a small group, students devise ways to transfer their own body weight "over each other." Some students would create wide, stable bases of support at varying levels. Additional students would maneuver over these bases of support utilizing transfer of weight from hands to feet. These movements could be connected with rolling actions, locomotor patterns, or various types of jumping actions.

Culminating Activity: Creating a Movement Sentence

Students, in small groups or individually, could then be prompted to create a "movement sentence" based on transfer of weight and incorporating as many of the movement concepts as possible. In this manner they are utilizing the information generated through exploration, experimentation, and observation at each of the five stations.

Conclusion

Educational gymnastics offers middle school students the opportunity to create movement patterns that assist in the refinement of basic locomotor and nonlocomotor skills. Lesson themes may be developed around any movement skill and may use a variety of equipment.

IDEAS III:

Section Five

Initiatives

Ice Breakers

By Kathy Ermler
Emporia State University
Emporia, KS

National Standards

🖉 Demonstrates responsible personal and social behavior in physical activity setting.
🖉 Demonstrates understanding and respect for differences among people in physical activity settings.
🖉 Understands that physical activity provides the opportunity for enjoyment, challenge, self-expression, and social interaction.

Introduction

Middle school is the time in which students are experiencing a new school building, new class scheduling, and new teachers. This is also a time when Students are meeting classmates from different elementary schools. As a result of these new experiences, students may feel uncomfortable and self-conscious when they interact with other students in a physical education class. The group initiatives that are listed below can help "break the ice" during the first two weeks of middle school.

Electric Fence

Divide the class into groups of six to eight students. The object of this initiative is to have the entire group get everyone over an electric fence without anyone touching the fence. The guidelines for this activity are:

✓ Tie a bungee cord or rope between two poles or trees at a height of about 3 ½ feet (about waist high). This rope is the "electric" fence.

✓ The group must stay connected to one another during the activity. Let the group determine the way they want to connect to each other. The connection cannot be made under the fence.

✓ If anyone in the group touches the electric fence or the connection among group members is broken, the entire group must start over.

Safety Tip. If this activity is done on a gym floor, make sure there are mats under the electric fence. Do not let students dive over the fence or roughly toss another group member over the fence.

Balloon Trolley

Divide the class into groups of five to six students. Give a balloon to each team member. Tell each student to blow his/her balloon up and tie it. The groups should then arrange themselves so that they have balloon between each person.

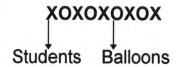

Once the students get in this position, they can only keep the balloon in place by pushing it into the person ahead of them. They may not use their hands to hold the balloon in place. The object of the activity is to be the first team to get from the starting line to the ending line with the balloons in place. If a team begins to lose a balloon, the group must stop and get the balloon back in place and then they can continue. If a balloon touches the floor, the group must start over again. To increase the difficulty of this initiative, have the first person tap his/her balloon in the air while the group makes their way across the area.

Pisa Lean

This activity should be used after the students are comfortable touching and being touched by other students. Divide the class into groups of 6-10 students. The groups should form a circle and stand shoulder to shoulder. The object is to lean toward the center of the circle, move their feet away from the center of the circle and maintain shoulder contact. They may not use their hands or arms to support the group.

Safety Tip. Make sure students do this activity on a matted or grassy area. If students start to fall, make sure they feel free to use their hands to catch other group members.

Down the Drain

This activity is great to use as a cool-down. Divide the class into groups of four or five students. Each student should have a plastic golf tube and each team should have one marble.

The teams line-up in single file with the first person in the line holding the marble. On a signal, the first person puts the marble into his/her tube. The second person runs to the front and connects tubes with the first person. The first person passes the marble to the second person. This process continues until the marble is carried over the finish line. The students must keep both hands in the middle of the golf tube. If the marble falls out, the team must start from the beginning.

Hand Flip

This activity encourages cooperation in a competitive activity. Divide the class into groups of 5-6 students. Each group should have one tennis ball. The object of the activity is for everyone in the group to volley the tennis ball without it hitting the ground.

To start the activity, have the groups form a semi-circle with one person standing in front of the group. The leader open hand volleys the ball to anyone standing in the semi-circle. At this point, the ball must be volleyed by everyone in the group and once a person touches it, he/she may not hit it again until everyone in the group has hit it.

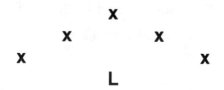

If the ball hits the ground before everyone touches it or if someone touches it twice, the leader gets a point and continues to serve. If the sequence is completed, no points are awarded to the leader and a new leader serves. Play until someone gets 11 points.

Conclusion

The activities performed during the first two weeks of middle school are critical to the formation of a cohesive group. The use of nonthreatening group initiatives is an excellent way to build trust, promote cooperation, and help the students to become familiar with each other.

Continuous Team Challenges

By Margie Miller
Skaith Elementary School
St. Joseph, MO

National Standards

- Demonstrates responsible personal and social behavior in physical activity settings.
- Demonstrates understanding and respect for differences among people in physical activity settings.
- Understands that physical activity provides the opportunity for enjoyment, challenge, self-expression, and social interaction.

Introduction

Team challenges are very popular with students. While each of these challenges can be done separately, they also may be combined for a continuous, on-going challenge that can be played over and over again for long periods of time. Students begin with puzzled looks, but these looks will give way to smiles and pride as they complete the challenges.

River Crossing

Equipment: Two scooters, one long rope, two deck tennis rings per group.

Group Size: Divide class into groups of 6 to 8 students per group. Set up several crossing stations along the river.

Description:

1. All group members must start on one side of the "river" (gym). All equipment should be on that side.
2. The task is to have all group members cross the river without any part of their body or clothing touching the "water' (gym floor). In addition, all equipment must also cross the river by the time the last person has crossed the river.
3. Rules:
   - The river is the area between the end line and midcourt line of a basketball court. If necessary, this area can be modified by using cones to mark the river bank boundaries.
   - If any part of a person's body or clothing touches the river, that person and another person who has crossed the river must start over.
   - The first person across the river cannot be sacrificed during the task.
   - There are no put downs or name calling.

The Rock

Equipment: One tumbling mat, tire, or hoop per group.

Group Size: Divide class into groups of 6 to 8 students per group.

Description

1. The task is for all group members to balance on the rock (tire) for a slow count of five.
2. Rules:
   - All group members must be off the floor but not necessarily touching the rock.
   - If anyone steps off the rock and touches the floor, even for an instant, the entire group must step off the rock and start again.
   - When the group is on the rock, they must signal the teacher.
   - The teacher witnesses the counting on the rock.

Continuous Team Challenges

- ***Set-up***. Set up the River Crossing and The Rock as stations. The Rock station should be set up directly on the other side of the River Crossing for each group. As soon as a group completes the River Crossing challenge, the group immediately goes to The Rock station and completes the task.

- ***New Challenges***. Once the group has completed The Rock, instruct them to-go back and cross the river again, but this time a different person must cross first and a different person must cross last. To make it more difficult, tell them to find a different way to cross than they previously used. Once a group has completed the River Crossing, pose a new challenge on The Rock. For example, the group must be balanced on the rock for a slow count of 10 seconds or they may only use seven points of contact on which to balance the entire group.

Conclusion

By adding new challenges each time a group completes the two initiatives, you will find that the students' enthusiasm increases for the tasks and they will want you to challenge them to complete harder and harder tasks. I have found that groups get very involved in solving their own particular challenge and seldom look around at other groups to see if they are "winning."

Getting the Most Out of Your Mats

By Jeff McAdoo
Quail Run Elementary
Lawrence, KS

National Standards

✎ Demonstrates responsible personal and social behavior in physical activity settings.
✎ Understands that physical activity provides the opportunity for enjoyment, challenge, self-expression, and social interaction.

Introduction

Folding mats are a standard piece of equipment in nearly every physical education program. They also are one the most costly, yet underused, pieces of equipment. After experimenting with the mats at our school, we found them to be one of the most valuable pieces of equipment for working on the life skills of teamwork, cooperation, creative problem solving, and communication.

Various mat challenges are listed below. Suggestions are provided that include safety considerations and ways to increase the difficulty level of the tasks and increase the challenge level for the students. We found that the more challenging the activity is to the students, the more fun and the more learning seems to take place.

Mat Challenges with Mats Flat on the Floor and Unfolded

Challenge 1

Groups of three or more must move the mat across gym. Students may touch the floor and must stay on top of the unfolded mat. Encourage them to watch others, take their ideas, but improve on them.

Challenge 2

Groups of three or more work together to spin the mat 180 or 360°. They must keep their entire bodies on top of the unfolded mat and keep the mat flat on the floor. Try having the students turn the mat upside down (top to bottom).

Challenge 3

Groups of three or more stand on a folded mat. They must unfold it without touching the floor. If they succeed in unfolding the mat, have the students refold the mat without touching the floor.

- Variation - Same as above, except students may use only their feet.

Challenge 4

"Fire and Snow, Stop, Drop, and Roll" - Lay all of the mats out in random fashion, with 1-3 feet between mats. Using multi-colored mats indicate that the red areas are the fire, the white areas are snow, the blue areas are water, and the floor is quick sand. Students continuously move anywhere they want to on the mats, avoiding the areas designated as "fire" and staying on other parts of the mats. If a student touches fire, he/she immediately goes to snow or water and "Stops, Drops, and Rolls." Encourage the students to be creative in how they get from one area to another. If they don't come up with it themselves, suggest doing a 180° as they jump from mat to mat or cartwheel from section to section.

Challenge 5

Groups of three or more students move across the gym using two mats. No one in the group can touch the floor.

Challenge 6

Groups of 10 or more students move across the gym using five mats. No one in the group can touch the floor. Once a mat has been used, it cannot be moved. Vary the number of mats according to the size of your gym. Start this with the mats folded and let students discover whether they want to unfold them or not.

Mat Challenges with Mats Upright on Edge

(Partially fold the mats in a "zig zag" fashion and they will stand upright. In this position they can be used as obstacles in games.)

Challenge 1

Tag games can be renewed as "Watch Out!" variations, by spreading several upright mats throughout the playing area. For most tag games the rules need not be changed. Caution the students to be careful when moving quickly around the mats. The ever present possibility of an opponent hiding behind a mat seems to make "Watch Out!" versions of tag games better than the original versions for working on agility.

Challenge 2

A "Great Wall" can be created by fastening several mats together with velcro. Many traditional games, such as volleyball, badminton, or other net games take on new life.

Challenge 3

Stand the mats on edge so that they are not very stable. In groups of four or more, have the students try to knock the mats over without touching them with anything.

Mat Challenges with Folded Mats

Challenge 1

Scooter Cars. In groups of two or more, three or four "scooters" under a folded mat to form a car or bus. Students stay on the mats in ways designated by the teacher and propel the mats in races or through obstacle courses.

Challenge 2

Log Rolls. Groups of four students or more lay down on the floor and place a folded mat on top of their bodies. They must move a folded mat by using their bodies as rolling logs under the mat. As the mat rolls past each person, he/she must get up quickly and move to the front of the mat, repeating this process until they reach their destination. Add heavier mats or riders on the mat to emulate the Egyptian pyramid builders moving blocks of stone.

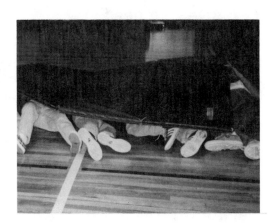

Challenge 3

Perimeter Obstacle Course. Place the folded mats around the perimeter of the gym. Stack the mats two to three high and vary the spaces between them. Part of the class can circle the gym, going up and down over the mats (or jumping from mat to mat) as a station while the rest of the class does other activities in the center of the gym. Balance beams, swinging ropes, and tunnels made with mats can be added to the obstacle course.

Mat Challenges While Carrying/Moving the Mats

Challenge 1

Groups of three or more student (depending on the size/weight of the mats and strength of the students) move their mat from one end of the gym to the other in various ways. Most of the ways can be designated either "...without the mat touching the floor," or " ... any safe way you can." Obstacles such as a "forest of poison" (Pringle cans or various "poison" balls spread out on the floor) can be used to increase the challenge. Indicate to the students that they need to find five different ways to get the mat to the opposite end of the gym with the mat in the positions listed below:

* Folded
* Unfolded
* Above your head
* Below the waist
* On edge
* Vertically (like a skyscraper)
* Without using the hands

Challenge 2

Elvis Concert. Students form a line across the gym. They must pass a mat from one side of the gym to the other without moving their feet. Let them do it anyway they want the first time. On the second effort, designate the position the mat must be passed (folded or unfolded) and time them on their effort. Have them try to beat their "world record" time. More than one mat can be passed to keep them active.

Challenge 3

Hammock. In groups 10 or more students, have one lie down in the middle of an unfolded mat. The other students stand along the sides of the mat and pick up the rider and the mat and carry them to the other end of the gym. The rider is replaced with another member of the group for the ride back. This process continues until all group members have had a ride.

Challenge 4

Surfing. Demonstrate the surfing position and then allow groups of three to five students to do this motion any safe way they choose on the mats. The easiest way to mat surf is to have one student stand on one end of a flat mat while the rest of the group pulls the mat and the surfer across the gym.

Mat Challenges While Carrying the Mats Over/Under Obstacles

Challenge 1

Stretch a rope across the gym about two feet above the floor. Groups of three or more students must move their mat from one side of the gym to the other without touching the "electric fence" with any part of their bodies, clothing, or the mat. Other possible challenges for this activity include:

* Mat goes over the rope, people go under.
* Move mat and students under fence without using the hands.
* Move mat over or under fence using only the feet.
* Move mat over or under fence while carrying an object or person on the mat.

Mat Challenges Using Mats and Carpet Squares

Challenge 1

Groups of three or more students move from one end of the gym to the other without touching the floor, using only two carpet pieces and carrying a mat.

Challenge 2

Large groups (even the whole class) use several carpet pieces to move several mats to the other end of the gym. The mats and the students may not touch the floor. Vary the number of carpet pieces to vary the difficulty.

Mat Challenges Using Connected or Stacked Mats

Challenge 2

Bulldozers. Using mats with velcro on the ends, fold or bend the mats and connect the ends of each mat so that it forms a continuous loop (like the tracks on a bulldozer). Two or more mats can be used to form a larger bulldozer, but try singles first. Students should remove their shoes and glasses. Individually or in groups of up to three students (depending on their size), get inside the bulldozers and find various ways to move it around the gym. **Caution:** This can get wild! Since people may be upside down or twisted together inside the mats, do not allow anyone to bulldoze over other bulldozers. After students get comfortable with this activity, add low balance beams, horizontal ladders, and various other obstacles up to about two feet high around the gym for them to bulldoze.

Challenge 2

Caterpillars. This is a bulldozer made with enough mats hooked together in a continuous loop that the entire class can get inside. The entire group must work together to get over obstacles too high for single bulldozers. The teacher can stipulate whether the students can stand inside the mats, or if they have to be side by side on their knees to make the caterpillar move.

Challenge 3

Using all the mats, the students must build a free standing structure. This could be done by allowing no external supports or allowing the use of a wall, a corner of two walls, basketball goals, etc. Students usually attempt to simply stack the mats while they are folded and then use some mats to stand on to reach higher. After their initial attempt, demonstrate how other ways to position the mats (on edge partially open in a zig zag fashion) can be used to build a taller structure. With good teamwork, students should be able to formulate a plan that allows them to build a much higher structure. One class found a way to build a tower over 20 feet high and their feet never left the floor!

Conclusion

Mat challenges can be used as warm-ups or as the main focus of the class period. Some of the more complicated challenges become lessons in perseverance and how to contend with failure. Encourage the students to be creative and not to judge the ideas of other students quickly. Teachers will find that these activities can be extremely useful in promoting problem-solving and decision-making skill.

IDEAS III:

Section Six

Special Events

Together in Fitness Day

By Jim Ross
Ridgewood Public Schools
Ridgewood, NJ

National Standards

✎ Exhibits a physically active lifestyle.
✎ Achieves and maintains a health-enhancing level of physical fitness.
✎ Understands that physical activity provides the opportunity for enjoyment, challenge, self-expression, and social interaction.

Introduction

Goal setting is an important element in improving student achievement and fostering teamwork and group cohesiveness. "Together in Fitness Day" is a district-wide special event that utilizes the strategies of goal setting in motivating students to achieve personal as well as group fitness goals. This event is simple to plan and organize. The necessary details of this event are listed below.

Pre-event Responsibilities (October)

1. *Individual School Responsibilities*

- Every student in each school in the district in the health-related fitness components of muscular strength, muscular endurance, cardiovascular endurance and flexibility.
- Record all scores for each student.

- Use the individual student's scores on each health-related component to establish a total school score. For example:

School 1
Curl-ups - 2,561
Pull-ups -   462
Sit and Reach - 876 cm
Mile Run - 623 minutes

School 2
Curl-ups - 2,701
Pull-ups -   350
Sit and Reach - 765 cm
Mile Run - 588 minutes

2. *District Responsibilities*

- Each school submits its scores and a total district-wide score is established. For example:

District Scores
Curl-ups - 6,862
Pull-ups - 1,245
Sit and Reach - 2,589 cm
Mile Run - 1,945 minutes

- Physical educators in the district should meet to establish fitness goals for the district.

Event (April or May)

1. *District Responsibilities*

- All students from all schools will meet at a common area (e.g.,
- park, school, field, etc.).
- Before students arrive at the site, teachers should set up stations for each of the health-related fitness components to be tested.

Physical Education Sure is Fun!!

- Include a fifth station (after the mile run) for water and cooperative activities.
- In an effort to create a "total team" atmosphere, mix students from different schools so each station has students from each school.
- Record scores without student names.
- Tabulate the scores and give the results to the students immediately.
- Challenge the students to improve the district's previous score established during the October pre-event.
- End the event with a total group cooperative activity (e.g., lap sit, knots, etc.).

Conclusion

"Together in Fitness Day" is a district-wide event that increases the motivation of students to develop and improve their fitness. Students are given a chance to assess their own personal levels of fitness, to establish goals, and to contribute to the overall school and district fitness score.

"World Famous" Jump Rope Unit

By John Smith
Ho-Ho-Kus Elementary School
Ho-Ho-Kus, NJ

National Standards

- Exhibits a physically active lifestyle.
- Achieves and maintains a health-enhancing level of physical fitness.
- Understands that physical activity provides the opportunity for enjoyment, challenge, self-expression, and social interaction.

Introduction

The Ho-Ho-Kus School's "World Famous" jump rope unit is now being used all over the United States, Europe, and the Far East. It is a simple, practical, no-frills unit in which every student in grades 3-12 can participate and be successful. This is a unit where there is a place for every kind of jump and jumper. The unit is flexible enough for every school to adapt it to its own situation and facilities.

Day 1: Record Setting Day 1

On this day all students try to set class, grade level, and school records in as many categories of jump roping as possible. (Save a few categories for Record Day 2). A bulletin board with the categories should be placed in a visible site. Teachers keep the records and supervise. Everything else is left up to the students. For a new record to go up on the board, a student must have someone count and verify the number. If a student has a new record, he/she comes to the board and announces it to the teacher: The student says "I have a new record. The category is _____. I did_____ jumps. My name is _____. The old record is erased and the new record is written in the box. This continues for the whole class period.

Day 2: Jump Rope Club Day

Place giant pieces of paper with jump rope skills and the number of jumps it takes to get into that club around the room. The students jump the rope and try to reach the level required to be a club member. If they reach that level, they sign their name on the paper.

Example:

Short Rope Forward Right Foot

| 10 | 20 | 40 | 75 | 100 |

(The names are signed under the number of jumps completed.)

Day 3: Evaluation Day and Fun Jump Day

On this day all students are given an evaluation on the basic jumps important in your curriculum. These may include jumping 1) short rope regular, 2) short rope backward, 3) short rope one foot, 4) long rope regular, and 5) long rope one foot. Students try to jump their grade level times 10 for a perfect score in each category. For example, for a third grader to get a perfect score on a jump, he/she would have to jump that particular jump 30 times (3 x 1 0).

The fun jumps include challenges such as 1) how many students in one rope, and 2) how many jumps with 2 five or more people. Different types of rope jumping such as 1) group turnstile, 2) egg beater, and 3) double Dutch can also be incorporated. Students may work with anyone in the class to attempt these jumps.

Day 4: Triplets

Challenges should be created that require groups of three students to jump using one, two, or three ropes. Each activity lasts three minutes. All three people must be part of the activity, but it is up to them to decide who does what. Sample challenges include:

⇨ Three in a long rope, one turns for all jumpers.
⇨ Three in a long rope, outsides turn the rope.
⇨ Two turning a long rope, one turns a short rope inside.
⇨ Two short ropes in a long rope, both turn own ropes, ropes hooked to wall.
⇨ Two in long rope, one turns for both, rope hooked to wall.
⇨ Two in long rope, both turn short rope, rope hooked to wall.
⇨ Two short ropes in long rope, front and back, ropes hooked to wall.

Day 5: Final Record Setting Day

This is the final attempt for the year at setting school records. These records will be published and kept for the year. We usually add a few more categories so that the numbers are not too high for the average jumper. These records are put in the school newspaper and on a bulletin board display. Students come back years later to see if their "school records" are still there.

Conclusion

Jump roping activities are very practical and simple to add to a middle school curriculum. The students will create new types of jumping patterns and skills if they are given the chance. This activity is also an excellent way to advertise your physical education programs.

DISC-ATHLON

By Sarah McCalister
Southern Illinois University
Carbondale, IL

National Standards

🖉 Applies movement concepts and principles to the learning and development of motor skills.
🖉 Understands that physical activity provides the opportunity for enjoyment, challenge, self-expression, and social interaction.

Introduction

Physical educators have begun to realize that the only way they can improve the fitness level of their students is to maximize their participation during physical education class. However, maximizing participation with large class sizes requires creative and innovative thinking. The disc-athlon is an affordable activity designed to promote maximum participation, as well as to provide an activity that is appropriate for all skill levels. The events in the disc-athlon can be made more challenging or simplified according to the needs and skill levels of the students. This aspect provides a great deal of flexibility for the teacher in terms of available space and equipment. The disc-athlon can be run as a competitive event where scores are recorded for each event or played as frisbee golf. It is an activity that can be utilized for one class period activity, multiple activity sessions, or a field day event.

The disc-athon provides the students with the opportunity to increase eye-hand coordination, enhance depth perception, and develop both fine and gross motor skills. In order to successfully throw a frisbee or disc, the students are required to have an understanding of angles and aerodynamics. For that reason, this activity also provides a wonderful avenue for teaching across the curriculum, especially in the areas of science and math.

Planning and Equipment

The events that comprise the disc-athlon are developed according to available equipment and space. Each student should have a disc in order to develop skill consistency. A disc can consist of competitive size frisbee or an inexpensive top off a butter tub. In designing the events, care should be taken so that all students have an equal chance of successfully completing the event.

If the physical educator desires the disc-athlon to be a competitive event, the stations should be developed with assigned point values for successful completion. If the goal is teaching across the curriculum, stations may be developed with academic questions and answers.

Events/Stations

1. **_Drop the Can_**. In this event, the student must sail the frisbee from behind a restraining line and toss it into a trash can. Points can be awarded on the basis of hitting the can within a specified number of throws or actually sailing the frisbee into the trash can. To modify this event it is possible to turn the can on its side and secure it. This requires the students to master a different type of frisbee delivery.

2. **_Nail the Goal_**. In order to successfully complete this event, the student  must sail the frisbee from behind a restraining line and hit a designated goal within a specified number of throws. Possible goals for this event might include goal posts, soccer goals, or archery targets. The archery targets provide special scoring options. The students can incorporate a number of math skills with the event or practice and reinforce archery scoring knowledge.

3. **_Set the Table_**. This event requires the students to sail the frisbee from behind a restraining line so that it lands on top of a table. As with other events, scoring should reflect the number of attempts. To increase the difficulty of this event the physical educator can require the students to bounce the frisbee from the ground onto the table. This added dimension requires the students to master a new type of frisbee delivery and can enhance learning of angles and aerodynamics.

4. ***Pierce the Hoop***. For this event, a hula-hoop needs to be suspended above so that it swings freely. Students stand behind a restraining line and attempt to sail the frisbee through the hoop. To increase the difficulty of this event simply add. a gentle swing to the hoop from side to side. The best scoring method for this event is to record the number of tries to a successful completion.

5. **Bowl Me Over**. Set up any formation of bowling pins, bottles, or Indian clubs. Students stand behind a restraining line and attempt to knock the pins over. This event can be scored in a number of different way. Students can take a certain number of throws and total up their score for the throws, or they can play a mini-bowling game and score four frames.

6. ***Slider***. Place two cones a foot apart and about 10 feet in front of the restraining line. Students must stand behind the line and attempt to slide the frisbee between the cones. Students should be instructed that successful completion of this event requires that the slide has to be the result of a throwing action and not pushing the frisbee across the floor. To modify this event, use a chair or bench and have the students slide the frisbee under it.

7. ***Come Back to Me***. The goal of this event is to sail the frisbee in such a way that the frisbee travels away and back to the thrower (similar to a boomerang). The easiest method of scoring this event is to establish boundary markers and require the frisbee to return close to the thrower.

Modifications

Many of these stations can be modified and expanded to enhance the value of frisbee as lifetime leisure activities. In terms of maximum participation, if each student has a frisbee, all students can be active at the same time. If the goal is cooperation, each event can be attempted through a partner or team effort. Partner work adds the aspects of catching skills and the development of strategy. In order to incorporate partner or team effort into the activity it is necessary to increase the distance to each individual goal. Also remember that the smaller the disc, the closer the restraining line needs to be to the target.

Conclusion

Frisbee activities provide an avenue for maximum participation which, in turn, leads to positive attitudes about physical education. Students are able to progress at their own speed and improve their physical skills in a nonthreatening activity. These activities also provide the physical educator with the opportunity to be creative and develop a unit that is fun and beneficial for students in a variety of areas.

Mini-Olympics

By Freda Blakley
Robidoux Middle School
St. Joseph, MO

National Standards

✎ Demonstrates competency in many movement forms and proficiency in a few movement forms.
✎ Applies movement concepts and principles to the learning and development of motor skills.
✎ Demonstrates responsible personal and social behavior in physical activity settings

Introduction

The purpose of the Mini-Olympics is to promote fitness through activities that encourage cooperation and fair play. It is an event that physical educators could use as the culminating event of fitness testing, as an end of the year playday, or as a parent/teacher back to school night activity.

Before the Mini-Olympics begins students are assigned to a team with 5 or 6 other students. Each team is assigned a country to represent during the event. In addition, students are informed about the symbols associated with the Olympic Games including the Olympic flag, motto, creed, oath, and torch.

The Mini-Olympics consists of several activities spread out over a two-day period. All the events listed on each day can be completed in a 50-minute class period. Equipment is kept to a minimum. The equipment needs for running the Mini-Olympics include: 3 stop watches, a 3-foot cageball, 6 frisbees and a target, 2 large folding mats, 2 basketballs, 2 bowling pins, and 10 bean bags. An example of a score card that can be used for the Mini-Olympics is in included at the end of this article.

Day One: Heptathlon Competition

The Heptathlon competition consists of seven events. Assign each team an event to begin the competition. After a designated time, teams will rotate to the next event.

Event 1: Globe Throw

Each team member will throw a cageball for distance. Take individual scores and add individual scores together for a team total in feet and inches.

Event 2: Foot Race - 4 x 50 Yard Relay

Each team member will run 50 yards and tag the next runner. Continue this process until every member of the team has run. Record team time in minutes and seconds.

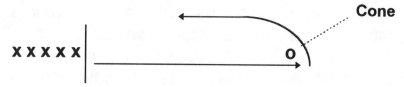

Cone

x x x x x   o

Event 3: Frisbee Toss

Each team member will toss six frisbees at a target from a designated area. Award a point for each successful toss into the target. Record individual scores and add scores together for a team total.

Event 4: Human Long Jump

Each team member will execute a standing long jump. Allow two jumps per person and record the best of the two jumps. Record individual scores and add scores together for a team total in feet and inches.

Event 5: Awesome Ab's

Each team member will execute abdominal curls on a mat. Students will count the number of curls completed in 60 seconds. All team members do curl-ups at the same time. Record individual scores and add scores together for a team total.

Event 6: 30-Second Shoot-Out

Each team member will attempt to make as many lay-ups into a basketball goal as possible in 30 seconds. Use two baskets and have students who are not shooting count for the shooters. Record individual scores and add scores together for a team total.

Event 7: Bag-a-Pin

Each team member will take turns using a bean bag to knock over a bowling pin. The bowling pin is placed about 10 feet away from the throwing area. Each person has five attempts to try to knock the pin over. Record the number of team members who are able to knock the pin over in five throws. (Once a person knocks the pin over, the next person goes.)

Day Two Pentathlon Competition:

The students remain on the same teams as the first day, and compete against other teams in the scooter relay races listed below. Before beginning these events, review scooter safety rules. These rules include:

- Tell your partner to slow down if you are going too fast.
- Let go of the rope if you are pulled off the scooter.
- Put your foot down on the floor to slow down or to stop your scooter.
- Keep your fingers away from the wheels of the scooter.
- Do not drag your partner on the floor.
- Do not interfere with other scooters.
- Never _stand_ on the scooters.
- If you lose your scooter, pick it up immediately and continue the race.

Event 1: American Crawl

Students must lie on their stomachs and use only their hands to propel the scooter to the end of the gym and back. Students then tag the next team member. Record the order of finish for each team.

Event 2: Back Stroke

Students must sit on the scooter and propel their bodies and scooter backward with their hands and feet. They go to the end of the gym and back, and tag the next team member. Record the order of finish for each team.

Event 3: Bob Sled

This event is a two-person competition in which Person A sits on two scooters (1 scooter for hip area and 1 scooter for the feet). Person B holds on to a looped end of the rope and pulls person A down to the end of the gym. At the end of the gym, the students switch places and Person B sits on the scooter and Person A pulls it back to the starting line. All team members must complete the task. Record the order of finish for each team.

Event 4: Wheelbarrow

This is a two person competition in which Person A lies on his/her stomach on two scooters. Person B pushes Person A down to the end of gym by only pushing on the feet. The students then switch places and Person B lies on the scooters and Person A pushes Person B back to the starting line. All team members must complete the task. Record the order of finish for each team.

Event 5: Canoe

All team members, must be seated on the scooters, and must be connected with each other. They may only use their hands to move down to the end of the gym and back. Record the order of finish for each team.

Conclusion

One of the most important concepts students should learn is the importance of taking part and trying their best, and not just the importance of winning. Each participant should receive a "gold" medal. These gold medals are simple to make and students are thrilled to receive them. The gold medals are made up of a piece of gold yarn with a gold Hershey's Kiss attached to the yarn. If you want to recognize individual or team winners, they can be give winner's certificates. You could also do collective class scores and have challenges among the various classes by posting class totals on the bulletin board in gymnasium.

Team Score Card

Globe Throw

Name	Distance
_____	_____
_____	_____
_____	_____
_____	_____
Team Total	_____

Human Long Jump

Name	Distance
_____	_____
_____	_____
_____	_____
_____	_____
Team Total	_____

30-Second Shoot-Out

Name	Number
_____	_____
_____	_____
_____	_____
_____	_____
Team Total	_____

Awesome Abs

Name	Number
_____	_____
_____	_____
_____	_____
_____	_____
Team Total	_____

Foot Race

Team Total _____

Frisbee Toss

Team Total Target _____

Bag-a-Pin

Team Total _____

Pentathlon	1st Place	2nd Place	3rd Place
American Crawl	_____	_____	_____
Back Stroke	_____	_____	_____
Bob Sled	_____	_____	_____
Wheelbarrow	_____	_____	_____
Canoe	_____	_____	_____

American Gladiators Revisited

By Joella Mehrhof
Emporia State University
Emporia, KS

National Standards

- Demonstrates responsible personal and social behavior in physical activity settings.
- Demonstrates understanding and respect for differences among people in physical activity settings.
- Understands that physical activity provides the opportunity for enjoyment, challenge, self-expression, and social interaction.

Introduction

American Gladiators helps students develop skills that are used in other sport activity areas, but above all it encourages cooperation and teamwork. Team members learn to depend on and help each other while competing in each event. The competition involves everyone in the class, and the excitement and fun of the team competition motivates students to improve their performances.

Procedures and Class Management

The class should be divided into two teams of 6-10 students each. Larger classes may have to be divided into four teams. The teams should be of comparable physical skill ability. The American Gladiators competition includes six events. Teams are awarded points for each event. The team with the highest point total at the end of the competition is declared the winner.

The events of the American Gladiators include Hang Over, Crossbar, Swedish Meatball, Air Bag, and Moon Ball. These events may be played in any order. The last event of the competition is The Eliminator.

After the teacher has explained the rules of an event, play begins. At the end of that event, the next event is explained and completed. This procedure continues until all of the events are completed.

Description of Events

Hang Over
Equipment needed: One large trash can, 50 beanbags, and a stopwatch

Description: The trash can is placed in the center of the running area. Team One players run clockwise, trying to toss bean bags over Team Two and into the trash can. Team Two runs counterclockwise, trying to keep Team One from getting the bean bags into the target. Bean bags that do not hit the target may be retrieved. Team One has 30 seconds to get as many beanbags into the trash can as possible. After 30 seconds the activity is repeated with Team Two as the offensive team. One point is given for each beanbag inside the trash can at the conclusion of the 30 seconds.

Safety: Both teams should run continually during the 30 seconds. Restraining circles need to be indicated. The throwing team is not allowed to enter these circles except to retrieve a beanbag.

Crossbar
Equipment: Low balance beam, 20 bean bags, a stopwatch

Description: One member from each team is designated to be the thrower. The thrower stands near the center of the beam and about 10 feet away and tosses bean bags to his/her team members as they move across the beam as quickly as possible. If a team member successfully catches the beanbag without failing off the beam and carries it to the end of the beam, the team is awarded one point. If a beanbag is dropped or if the person falls off the beam, no points are recorded. Points earned should be added to that team's total. Each team is given 45 seconds to complete the activity.

Safety: Only one team member may be on the beam at a time.

Swedish Meatball

Equipment: 5 large trash cans, 2 baskets or ball racks, 40 balls (volleyballs, basketballs, playground balls, etc.)

Description: Five large trash cans serve as goals. The baskets or ball racks serve as retrieving stations, with half of the balls in each basket. Team One tries to get as many balls into the trash cans as possible. Team Two tries to keep Team One from getting the balls into the trash cans. Points are scored when a ball is successfully placed in a trash can. The corner trash cans are worth one point, while the center trash can is worth three points. Points earned should be added to the respective team point total. Each team has 30 seconds to complete the activity.

Safety: Team members may have only one ball in their hands at a time. Once a ball is dropped it may not be retrieved for scoring. Neither team may push, tackle, or slap members of the opposing team, or hang/lay on the trash cans.

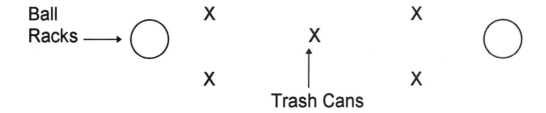

Air Bag

Equipment: 50 beanbags, a stopwatch

Description: Team One stands inside a designated area which is about the size of a free-throw lane. Team Two stands around the area and about 10 feet away. Team Two throws beanbags at the feet of the members of Team One, who are jumping and trying to stay off the ground. The only time a hit is counted is when a player's feet are on the ground. The teacher should count the total number of hits for each team. Points should be added to the running tally for each team. Each team is given 30 seconds to complete the activity. Teams trade places after 30 seconds.

Safety: Students should be told to aim the beanbags at the feet of the opponents and no higher. If the feet are in the air, the hit with the beanbag does not count.

Moon Ball

Equipment: 20 volleyballs

Description: All team members lie on their backs in a circle with heads toward the center of the circle. The team tries to pass volleyballs as quickly as possible around the circle using only the feet of the participants. Both teams may do the activity at the same time. A team will score one point for each volleyball that is passed completely around the circle. Points earned should be added to the respective team's total. The time limit for this activity is two minutes.

Safety: Each team should have a feeder who places the volleyball onto the feet of the first team member. If a ball is dropped, it is considered dead and may not be recovered.

The Eliminator

Equipment: 2 scooters, long jump rope, 12 cones, 10 balloons, vaulting box, 15 hula hoops, a bench

Description: The Eliminator is the final event. It is an add-on event. A team member is stationed at each new task. Team member number one starts and completes task one (order shown below). This person then joins a hand with team member number two to complete task number two. They will then join with team member number three and complete task number three. This continues until all team members are connected in a single line with hands joined. At this point in the American Gladiator competition, the team that has the least amount of accumulated points should be allowed to perform The Eliminator last. The opponents will compete in The Eliminator when the first team has completed all tasks. The team that completes The Eliminator fastest is awarded eight points. The second fastest team is given four points. The event is timed. Time stops when participants have completed all tasks and have crossed the finish line.

<u>Safety</u>: Team members perform with joined hands. If at any time the grasps are lost, the team members must stop and regrasp immediately.

<u>Task Order:</u>

1. Push-ups
2. Ride scooters to half court
3. Jump rope five times
4. Zig zag maze (made from cones)
5. Pop 5 balloons
6. Go over the vault
7. Run through a hula hoop maze
8. Sit-ups
9. Crawl under a bench
10. Run a lap

Conclusion

American Gladiators can be a cooperative as well as a competitive activity. Outside of the classroom, this activity can be used as a fun way to condition athletic teams during pre-season and off-season. This activity can be used in intramural programs as well as in parent participation evenings.

ABOUT THE CONTRIBUTING AUTHORS

FREDA BLAKLEY is the physical educator at Robidoux Middle School in St. Joseph, Missouri. Ms. Blakley was the 1995 Missouri Middle School Physical Educator of the Year.

WENDELL BROWN is an assistant principal at Dunbar Junior High in Lubbock, Texas. Mr. Brown was the Texas Secondary Physical Educator of the Year in 1992.

FRAN CLELAND is a dance and physical educator at West Chester University in West Chester, Pennsylvania. Dr. Cleland has served on numerous professional committees at the state, regional, and national levels.

PAUL DARST is a professor in the Department of Exercise Science and Physical Education at Arizona State University in Tempe, Arizona. Dr. Darst is one of the authors of *Dynamic Physical Education for Secondary School Students* published by Allyn and Bacon.

MEGGIN DEMOSS is the physical educator at Seltzer Elementary School in Wichita, Kansas. Ms. DeMoss was the 1996 Kansas Elementary Physical Educator of the Year.

MICHELLE DILISIO is the physical education teacher at Chanute High School in Chanute, Kansas. Ms. DiLisio was the 1996 Central District Secondary Physical Educator of the Year.

DON HICKS is the physical education director of the Fort Worth Country Day School in Fort Worth, Texas. Mr. Hicks was the 1990 Arizona Elementary Physical Educator of the Year.

JEFF MCADOO is a physical educator at Quail Run Elementary in Lawrence, Kansas. Mr. McAdoo has presented his unique ideas at many conferences and workshops.

SARAH McCALISTER is an assistant professor in the Department of Physical Education at Southern Illinois University at Carbondale. Dr. McCalister taught at the secondary level for several years before earning her doctorate and moving to the university teaching level.

SANDY MENELEY is a physical educator at Landon Middle School in Topeka, Kansas. Ms. Meneley has served on NAPSE's Middle and Secondary School Physical Education Council.

MARGIE MILLER is a physical educator at Skaith Elementary in St. Joseph, Missouri. Dr. Miller was the 1995 Missouri Elementary Physical Educator of the Year.

ROBERT PANGRAZI is a professor in the Department of Exercise Science and Physical Education at Arizona State University in Tempe, Arizona. Dr. Pangrazi is the author of several books and articles on the teaching of physical education.

PUG PARRIS is a professor in Department of Physical Education at McMurry University in Abilene, Texas. Dr. Parris was the recipient of the 1990 Sears Teaching Excellence Award and is presently the President-Elect for the Texas AHPERD.

RICKEY PARRIS is the physical educator and coach at Mann Middle School in Abilene, Texas. Mr. Parris has been inducted into the NAIA Track Hall of Fame.

JIM ROSS is a physical educator with the Ridgewood Public Schools Ridgewood, New Jersey. Mr. Ross was the 1995 Eastern District Elementary Physical Educator the Year.

JOHN SMITH is a physical educator with the Ho Ho Kus Public Schools Ho Ho Kus, New Jersey. Mr. Smith was the 1989 NASPE National Elementary Physical Educator of the Year.

MARK STANBROUGH is an assistant professor in the Division of Health, Physical Education, and Recreation at Emporia State University in Emporia, Kansas. Dr. Stanbrough is the author *Lifetime Fitness* published by Kendall Brown Publishers.

BELINDA STILLWELL is a doctoral student in the Department of Exercise Science and Physical Education at Arizona State University in Tempe, Arizona. Ms. Stillwell taught in the public school system in Los Angeles, California, before beginning her doctoral studies.

SUE TILLERY is the physical educator at Rockwood Valley Middle School in Manchester, Missouri. Ms. Tillery was the 1994 NASPE Middle School Physical Educator of the Year.

NANNETTE WOLFORD is an assistant professor in the Department of Physical Education and Leisure Studies at Missouri Western State College in St. Joseph, Missouri. Dr. Wolford has served as a NASPE Physical Best consultant for several years.

LINDA WILKINS is the director of FiTrain in Acworth, Georgia. Ms. Wilkins has presented at numerous national conferences and school district workshops.

NASPE Guidelines for
Middle School Physical Education

THE MIDDLE SCHOOL

The current concept of the middle school began in the late 1950s and emerged as a popular alternative to the junior high school. The rationale supporting the middle school philosophy is based on a concern for the special needs and interests of 10-to-14-year-old students and the failure of the junior high school to meet the needs of children of this age.

Program Characteristics

The middle school program is designed to provide variations in instructional modalities to meet the different learning styles and developmental rates of middle-school-aged youth. The middle school program should be I-/ characterized by:

1. A home base and teacher for every student, to provide the continuing guidance and assistance to help students with daily decision making.
2. Balanced learning opportunities addressing the three major goals of the middle school: (a) personal development of the between-ager, (b) continued learning skills, and (c) effective use of appropriate knowledge.
3. An instructional design focused on individual progress, with many curricular options and with individualized instruction in appropriate areas.
4. The use of interdisciplinary team arrangement for cooperative planning, instructing, and evaluating.
5. A wide range of exploratory activities that promote socialization, develop interest, and enrich leisure time.

Characteristics of Middle School Students

It is difficult to describe or categorize the clientele of the middle school in a concise statement. This period of transition is one of stresses and strains, of upheaval in the physical, emotional, social, and intellectual worlds. This is a period of great physical change, of uneven growth, of wide variations among children in height, weight, and physical maturity. The following descriptors help us understand the characteristics of the middle school student.

Physically:
- Needs to master a new physical body that may experience great physical change and uneven growth.
- Faces the task of gender role identification.
- May experience a sense of physical inadequacy.

Emotionally:
- Tries to cope with physical and hormonal changes that provoke feelings of love, fear, and anger.
- Needs to establish a positive self-concept.
- Needs success and recognition as an individual.

Socially:
- Seeks peer acceptance and approval.
- Needs to establish a personal value system.
- Needs guidance to establish independence.
- Needs to belong to a group.

Intellectually:
- Is responsive to new ideas and experiences.
- Has a new intellectual prowess.
- Can now handle abstract concepts.

The above characteristics, though not unique to the middle-school-aged youth tend to be more apparent in middle school children. Regardless of these students' ability level, educational situations should be structured to meet their specific needs. It is believed that physical education in the middle school can help students develop an understanding of their changing bodies and personalities and how these changes affect their relationships with others.

GOALS OF THE INSTRUCTIONAL PROGRAM

The Physical Education Outcomes Committee of the National Association for Sport and Physical Education was charged with the responsibility to define the "physically educated student", (i.e., the desired characteristics of students who complete appropriately designed and conducted school physical education programs). The Committee (1991) has completed a definition of the physically educated student and has identified the outcomes that clarify and amplify this definition. For each of the five parts of the definition (HAS, IS, DOES, KNOWS, VALUES) there 20 attendant outcomes. Benchmarks were also developed for grades K, 2, 4, 6, 8, 10, and 12, but will not be identified in this document. The benchmarks suggest when assessment might occur and what might be assessed.

A Physically Educated Person:

- **HAS learned skills necessary to perform a variety of physical activities.**

1. . . .moves using concepts of body awareness, space awareness, effort, and relationships.
2. . . .demonstrates competence in a variety of manipulative, locomotor, and non-locomotor skills.
3. . . .demonstrates competence in combinations of manipulative, locomotor, and non-locomotor skills performed individually and with others.
4. . . .demonstrates competence in many different forms of physical activity.
5. . . .demonstrates proficiency in a few forms of physical activity.
6. . . .has learned how to learn new skills.

- **IS physically fit.**

7. . . .assesses, achieves, and maintains physical fitness.
8. . . .designs safe, personal fitness programs in accordance with principles of training and evaluation.

- **DOES participate regularly in physical activity.**

9. . . . participates in health-enhancing physical activity at least three times a week.
10 . . . selects and regularly participates in lifetime physical activities.

- **KNOWS the implications of and the benefits from involvement in physical activities.**

11. . .identifies the benefits, costs, and obligations associated with regular participation in physical activity.
12. . .recognizes the risk and safety factors associated with regular participation in physical activity.
13. . .applies concepts and principles to the development of motor skills.
14. . .understands that wellness involves more than being physically fit.
15. . .knows the rules, strategies, and appropriate behaviors for selected physical activities.
16. . .recognizes that participation in physical activity can lead to multicultural/international understanding.
17. . .understands that physical activity provides the opportunity for enjoyment, self-expression, and communication.

- **VALUES physical activity and its contribution to a healthful lifestyle.**

18. . . .appreciates the relationships with others that result from participation in physical activity.
19. . . .respects the role that regular physical activity plays in the pursuit of life-long health and well being.
20. . . .cherishes the feelings that result from regular participation in physical activity.

THE CURRICULUM

Physical activity programs should be comprehensive and well balanced for the purpose of enhancing the psychomotor, cognitive, and affective development of individuals through the means of body movement. It has been long recognized that middle school students need quality physical experiences on a regular basis. The unique contribution of movement to the development of youth indicates that the middle school curriculum should provide for systematic instruction in a wide variety of activities. These offerings should include activities and concepts in the areas of conditioning and physical fitness, individual and dual sports, team sports, gymnastics, rhythms, and dance, track and field, aquatics, and outdoor activities.

These physical education experiences must be planned and implemented in ways that will maximize the potential contribution to the overall goals of education. Basic concepts in physical education should be identified and integrated through a wide variety of activities. Therefore, it is believed that middle school physical activity programs should:

- Allow students to participate in physical education on a regular basis equivalent to five times per week.
- Have philosophy and program goals consistent with the educational goals of the school system and that reflect the needs of middle school students.
- Represent a transitional progression from the elementary program to the high school program by providing the opportunity to participate in short exploratory units as well as longer units of instruction.
- Have specific instructional objectives for each activity.
- Have each activity developed on a continuum so that students can progress on an individual basis.
- Provide a variety of physical education activities for all students regardless of their level of physical development.
- Allow students to assess and evaluate their physical and social selves.
- Provide opportunities for the remediation of motor and fitness skills.
- Provide experiences that will promote motor skill development and fitness.
- Provide opportunities for students to be more self-directing in the selection of and performance in activities.

- Reflect a multi-media, multi-space approach with opportunities for individual learning in skill acquisition and fitness development.
- Provide for interaction and coordination with other disciplines in the school curriculum.
- Provide the concepts and skills to pursue personal wellness for a lifetime. Develop skills that will enable them to apply technology to the development personal wellness.
- Develop an appreciation of physical activity and its effect on total well being.

THE TEACHER

Preparation of teachers should include courses and teaching experiences that pertain to the education of middle school students. The in-service education program for physical education teachers is imperative to assure skilled and knowledgeable teachers to administer the varied program required for middle schools. Administrative support is necessary to encourage and to provide opportunities to attend workshops, meetings, and conventions that keep physical education personnel current on materials and information.

Educational programs should prepare teachers who:

- Have an understanding of the middle school concept.
- Possess teaching certification in physical education.
- Avoid gender role discrimination and gender stereotyping by grouping students according to interest and ability levels.
- Understand the physical, social, emotional, and intellectual characteristics that are unique to middle school youth.
- Possess a positive self-concept and demonstrate respect for the dignity and worth of all individuals.
- Have knowledge and skills of developmentally appropriate practices to work with students on a one-to-one basis.
- Are familiar with a wide variety of skills and activities in order to implement the exploratory qualities of the program.
- Apply various teaching styles and modify rules, equipment, and instructional stations to conform to the needs of the learner.
- Continually strive to increase their knowledge and understanding to meet the changing needs of middle school students and their learning environment.
- Can interact with students and fellow teachers in a way that is supportive of the special needs of the middle school student.
- Will assume leadership in providing for the expanded physical activity experiences for all students in the school.

- Are able to interpret the goals and objectives of the activity programs to students and their parents.
- Use instructional strategies based upon the developmental and skill levels of the student as well as the nature of the activity.
- Are able to maintain and manage record keeping systems for planning sequential instruction.

MEASUREMENT AND EVALUATION

Measurement involves the systematic collection of data. Evaluation is the process of interpreting data for individual students and the overall program. Achievement of course and program objectives should be measured and curricular decisions should be based on the evaluation of the information gathered. The recommendations listed below provide a process of measurement and evaluation to assess knowledge, learning, and experience in physical education. The process of measurement and evaluation should be a means of helping students to further realize their potential. It should also help educators to evaluate and direct programs.

- Evaluation of students within the psychomotor, cognitive, and affective domains should be based on valid, reliable, and objective measurement.
- Formative evaluation of students should provide progress of student learning in relation to selected individualized criteria.
- Summative evaluation of students should assist in grading.
- Evaluation of students' performance should serve as a guide to instructional planning.
- Evaluative criteria should be criterion-based and focus on changes in an individual's performance.
- Program evaluation should be used as a means of interpreting the physical education program to school and community.
- Program evaluation should serve as an indicator of quality of instruction.

Source: *Guidelines for Middle School Physical Education.* NASPE, 1992.

National Standards for Physical Education

Demonstrates competency in many movement forms and proficiency in a few movement forms.

The intent of this standard is the development of movement competence and proficiency. Movement competence implies the development of sufficient ability to enjoy participation in physical activities and establishes a foundation to facilitate continued motor skill acquisition and increased ability to engage in appropriate motor patterns in daily physical activities. The development of proficiency in a few movement forms gives the student the capacity for successful and advanced levels of performance to further increase the likelihood of participation. In the primary years students develop maturity and versatility in the use of fundamental skills (e.g., running, skipping, throwing, striking) that are further refined, combined and varied during the middle school years. These motor patterns, now having evolved into specialized skills (e.g., a specific dance step, chest pass, catching with a glove) are used in increasingly more complex movement environments (e.g., more players or participants, rules, and strategies) through the middle school years. On the basis of interest and ability, high school students select a few activities for regular participation within which proficiency will be developed. In preparation for adulthood, students should have acquired the basic skills to participate in a wide variety of leisure and work-related physical activities and advanced skills in at least two or three areas.

Applies movement concepts and principles to the learning and development of motor skills.

This standard concerns the ability of the learner to use cognitive information to understand and enhance motor skill acquisition and performance. This includes the application of concepts from disciplines such as motor learning and development, sport psychology and sociology, biomechanics, and exercise physiology. Specifically this would include concepts like increasing force production through the summation of forces, effects of anxiety on performance, and the principle of specificity of training. Knowledge of such concepts and practice applying these concepts enhances the likelihood of independent learning and therefore more regular and effective participation in physical activity. During the lower elementary years emphasis is placed on establishing a movement vocabulary and initial application of introductory concepts (e.g., force absorption, principles governing equilibrium, application of force). Through the upper elementary and middle school years an emphasis is placed on learning more and increasingly complex concepts. In addition, emphasis is placed on applying and generalizing these concepts to real life physical activity situations (e.g., managing stress, effect of growth spurt on movement performance). During the high school years the student should possess sufficient knowledge of concepts to independently and routinely use a wide variety of increasingly complex concepts (e.g., performance trends associated with learning new motor skills, specificity of training). By graduation the student should have developed sufficient knowledge and ability to independently use their knowledge to acquire new skills while continuing to refine existing ones.

Exhibits a physically active lifestyle.

The intent of this standard is to establish patterns of regular participation in meaningful physical activity. This standard should connect what is done in the physical education class with the lives of students outside of physical education. While participation within the physical education class is important, what the student does outside the physical education class is critical to developing an active, healthy lifestyle. Students are more likely to participate if they have had opportunities to develop interests that are personally meaningful to them. Young children should learn to enjoy physical activity. They should participate in developmentally appropriate activities that help them develop movement competence and they should be encouraged to participate in vigorous and unstructured play. As students get older the structure of activity tends to increase and the opportunities for participation in different types of activity increase outside of the physical education class. Attainment of this standard should develop an awareness of those opportunities and encourage a broad level of participation. Cognitive understandings develop from an initial awareness of cause and effect relationships between activity and its immediate and identifiable effects on the body to an increased understanding of the role of physical activity on the physiological body, social opportunities and relationships, and emotional well being; and a comprehensive perspective on the meaning of the idea of a healthy lifestyle.

Achieves and maintains a health-enhancing level of physical fitness.

The intent of this standard is for the student to achieve a health-enhancing level of physical fitness. Students should be encouraged to develop higher levels of basic fitness and physical competence as needed for many work situations and active leisure participation. Health-related fitness components include cardiorespiratory endurance, muscular strength and endurance, flexibility, and body composition. Expectations for students' fitness levels should be established on a personal basis, taking into account variation in entry levels, rather than setting a single standards for all children at a given grade level. For elementary children, the emphasis is on an awareness of fitness components and having fun while participating in health-enhancing activities that promote physical fitness. Middle school students gradually acquire a greater understanding of the fitness components, how each is developed and maintained, and the importance of each in overall fitness. Secondary students are able to design and develop an appropriate personal fitness program that enables them to achieve desired levels of fitness. The student thus should have both the ability and willingness to accept responsibility for personal fitness leading to an active, healthy lifestyle.

Demonstrates responsible personal and social behavior in physical activity settings.

The intent of this standard is achievement of self-initiated behaviors that promote personal and group success in activity settings. These include safe practices, adherence to rules and procedures, etiquette, cooperation and teamwork, ethical behavior in sport, and positive social interaction. Achievement of this standard in the lower elementary grades begins with recognition of classroom rules and procedures and a focus on safety. In the upper elementary levels, students learn to work independently, with a partner, and in small groups. In the middle school, students identify the purposes for rules and procedures and become involved in decision making processes to establish rules and procedures for specific activity situations. High school students initiate responsible behavior, function independently and responsibly, and positively influence the behavior of others in physical activity settings.

Demonstrates understanding and respect for differences among people in physical activity settings.

The intent of this standard is to develop respect for individual similarities and differences through positive interaction among participants in physical activity. Similarities and differences include characteristics of culture, ethnicity, motor performance, disabilities, physical characteristics (e.g., strength, size, shape), gender, race, and socioeconomic status. Elementary school students begin to recognize individual similarities and differences and participate cooperatively in physical activity. By middle school, students participate cooperatively in physical activity with persons of diverse characteristics and backgrounds. High school students are expected to be able to participate with all people, recognize the value of diversity in physical activity, and develop strategies for inclusion of others.

Understands that physical activity provides opportunities for enjoyment, challenge, self-expression, and social interaction.

This standard is designed to develop an awareness of the intrinsic values and benefits of participation in physical activity that provides personal meaning. Physical activity can provide opportunity for self-expression and social interaction and can be enjoyable, challenging, and fun. These benefits entice people to continue participation in activity throughout the life span. Elementary school children derive pleasure from movement sensations and experience challenge and joy as they sense a growing competence in movement ability. At the middle school level participation in physical activity provides important opportunities for challenge, social interaction, and group membership, as well as opportunities for continued personal growth in physical skills and their applied settings. Participation at the high school level continues to provide enjoyment and challenge as well as opportunities for self-expression and social interaction. As a result of these intrinsic benefits of participation, students will begin to actively pursue lifelong physical activities that meet their own needs.

Source: *Moving Into The Future: National Standards for Physical Education*, NASPE, 1995.

NASPE PHYSICAL EDUCATION OUTCOMES PROJECT

EXAMPLES OF BENCHMARKS - SIXTH GRADE

As a result of participating in a quality physical education program it is reasonable to expect that the student will be able to:

HAS	FUND MOVE	1.	Leap, roll, balance, transfer weight, bat, volley, hand and foot dribble, and strike a ball with a paddle, using a mature motor pattern.
HAS	MOVE FORM	2.	Demonstrate proficiency in front, back, and side swimming strokes.
HAS	MOVE FORM	3.	Design and perform gymnastics and dance sequences that combine traveling, rolling, balancing, and weight transfer into smooth, flowing sequences with intentional changes in direction, speed, and flow.
HAS	MOVE FORM	4.	Design and refine a routine combining various jump rope movements to music so that it can be repeated without error.
HAS	FUND SKILL	5.	Consistently strike a ball, so that it travels in an intended direction and height, using a golf club and hockey stick.
HAS	FUND SKILL	6.	Consistently throw and catch a ball while guarded by opponents.
HAS	FUND SKILL	7.	Throw a variety of objects demonstrating both accuracy and distance, (e.g., frisbees, deck tennis rings, footballs).
HAS	FUND SKILL	8.	Continuously strik4 a ball to a wall, or a partner, with a paddle using both forehand and backhand strokes.
HAS	FUND SKILL	9.	In a small group keep an object continuously in the air without Catching it, (e.g., ball, foot bag).
HAS	FUND SKILL	10.	Hand dribble and foot dribble and prevent an opponent from stealing the ball.
HAS	FUND SKILL	11.	Design and play small-group games that involve cooperating with others to keep an object way from opponents (basic offensive and defensive strategies - e.g.- by throwing, kicking and/or dribbling a ball).
IS	AEROBIC	12.	Monitor heart rate before, during, and after activity.
IS	AEROBIC	13.	Participate in vigorous activity for a sustained period of time while maintaining a target heart rate.
IS	AEROBIC	14.	Recover from vigorous physical activity in an appropriate length of time.
IS	HEA FIT	15.	Correctly demonstrate activities designed to improve and maintain muscular strength and endurance, flexibility, and cardiorespiratory functioning.
DOES	PART/ACT	16.	Experience games, sports, dance, and outdoor pursuits, both in and outside of school, based on individual interests and capabilities.
KNOWS	COMMUNICATE	17.	Describe ways to use the body and movement activities to communicate feelings.
KNOWS	FUND SKILL	18.	Detect, analyze, and correct errors in personal movement patterns.
KNOWS	HEA FIT	19.	Identify proper warm-up, conditioning, and cool-down techniques and the reasons for using them.
KNOWS	MOVE FORM	20.	Recognize the role of games, sports, and dance in getting to know and understand others of like and different cultures.
KNOWS	PART/ACT	21.	Identify opportunities in the school and community for regular participation in physical activity.

KNOWS RISK	22.	Evaluate the time and effort needed to be given to practice if skill improvement and fitness benefits are to be realized.
VALUESRISK	23.	Identify benefits resulting from participation in different forms of physical activities.
VALUES DIFF/OTHER	24.	Seek out, participate with, and show respect for persons of like and different skill levels.
VALUES HEA FIT	25.	Choose to exercise at home for personal enjoyment and benefit.
VALUES RULES	26.	Accept and respect the decisions made by game officials, whether they are fellow students, teachers, or officials outside of school.

NASPE PHYSICAL EDUCATION OUTCOMES PROJECT

EXAMPLES OF BENCHMARKS - EIGHTH GRADE

As a result of participating in a quality physical education program it is reasonable to expect that the student will be able to:

HAS	FUND SKILL	1.	Practice in ways that are appropriate for helping them learn new skills or sports on their own.
HAS	MOVE FORM	2.	Perform a variety of simple folk, square, and creative dances.
HAS	MOVE FORM	3.	Use basic offensive and defensive strategies in modified net games, (e.g., tennis, volleyball, badminton) and invasive games, (e.g., soccer, basketball).
HAS	MOVE FORM	4.	Combine skills competently to participate in modified versions of team and individual sports, (e.g., soccer, racquetball, tennis, golf).
HAS	MOVE FORM	5.	Demonstrate track and field skills.
HAS	MOVE FORM	6.	Explore introductory outdoor pursuit skills, (e.g. backpacking, rock climbing, hiking, canoeing, cycling, ropes courses).
IS	AEROBIC	7.	Sustain an aerobic activity, maintaining a target heart rate to achieve cardiovascular benefits.
IS	BODYCOMP	8.	Achieve and maintain appropriate body composition.
IS	STRENGTH	9.	Perform activities requiring muscular endurance.
IS	ENDURANCE	10.	Correctly demonstrate various weight lifting techniques.
IS	STRENGTH	11.	Demonstrate muscular strength to control body during physical activity.
IS	HEA FIT	12.	Participate in an individualized fitness program.
DOES	FIT PLAN	13.	Participate in an individualized fitness program.
DOES	RULES	14.	Apply rules and courtesies in physical activities.
KNOWS	HEA FIT	15.	Describe principles of training and conditioning for specific physical activities.
KNOWS	HEA FIT	16.	Analyze and categorize activities and exercises according to potential fitness benefits.
KNOWS	HEA FIT	17.	Evaluate the roles of exercise and other factors in weight control.
KNOWS	MOVE FORM	18.	Analyze offensive and defensive strategies in games and sports.
KNOWS	MOVE FORM	19.	Recognize appropriate performance-altering practices.
KNOWS	RULES	20.	Describe personal and group conduct appropriate for engaging in physical activity.
KNOWS	VAL/BENEFIT	21.	List long-term physiological, psychological, and cultural benefits that may result from regular participation in physical activity.
KNOWS	VAL/ETHICS	22.	Discuss ethical and unethical behavior during participation in physical activity.
KNOWS	AESTHETIC	23.	Derive satisfaction in the aesthetic and creative aspects of performance.
VALUES	DIFF/OTHER	24.	Respect physical limitations of self and others.
VALUES	FEEL	25.	Feel dissatisfied on days when they do not engage in physical activity.
VALUES	SKILL DEV	26.	Desire to improve physical ability and performance.

Source: *Outcomes of Quality Physical Education Programs*, NASPE, 1992.

Resources

Published by NASPE/AAHPERD to support quality physical education programs. Available for purchase by calling 1-800-321-0789.

AAHPERD. *Physical Best*, 1989. Guide to fitness education.

Carlson, R. *Ideas II: A Sharing of Teaching Practices by Secondary School Physical Education Practitioners*, 1984.

Cooper Institute for Aerobics Research (CIAR). *Prudential Fitnessgram.* Assessment of health-related physical fitness. TO ORDER CALL (800)635-7050.

Dougherty, N., Ed. *Principles of Safety in Physical Education and Sport*, 1993. Complements *Physical Activity and Sport for the Secondary School Student.*

Dougherty, N., Ed. *Physical Activity and Sport for the Secondary School Student*, 1993.

NASPE. *Appropriate Practices for Middle School Physical Education*, 1995.

NASPE. *Appropriate Practices for High School Physical Education*, 1996.

NASPE. *Developmentally Appropriate Physical Education Practices for Children*, 1992.

NASPE. *Including Students with Disabilities in Regular Physical Education*, 1995.

NASPE. *Looking at Physical Education from a Developmental Perspective: A Guide to Teaching*, 1994.

NASPE. *Moving into the Future: National Standards for Physical Education, A Guide to Content and Assessment*, 1995.

NASPE. *Outcomes of Quality Physical Education Programs*, 1992.

NASPE. *Program Guidelines and Appraisal Checklists for School Physical Education Programs.*
> Elementary School, revised 1994.
> Middle School, revised 1992.
> Secondary School, revised 1992.

NASPE, *Sport and Physical Education Advocacy Kit (SPEAK),* 1994.

Rink, J. *Critical Crossroads*, 1993. Covers three areas of secondary physical education: curriculum, instruction, and assessment/evaluation.

Roberts, S. *Developing Strength in Children: A Comprehensive Guide*, 1996.